Love Makes the Word Go Round

Keith Huttenlocker

 WARNER PRESS

Anderson, Ind.

Library of Congress Cataloging in Publication Data
Huttenlocker, Keith
Love makes the word go round

  1. Love (Theology) 2. Christian life —
Church of God authors. I. Title.
BV4639.H89   248'.48'673   73-21613
ISBN 0-87162-170-3

Printed in the United States of America

All Scripture passages are from the King James Version or the Revised Standard Version unless otherwise noted

PUBLISHER'S PREFACE

Christian love makes possible the continuance and spread of the church, the body of Christ and the community of Christian love. It is from the standpoint of love that this book comes at an emphasis on the church, its life and mission, which is being widely examined in congregations. A common emphasis or perspective for study at all age levels in many congregations is "When We Are the Church." This book serves to undergird that emphasis across age lines by surveying the biblical and doctrinal backgrounds associated with love as the binding and energizing force in Christian community. The book may be used for adult Sunday school classes, for teacher training courses, and for individual reading and reflection.

The book comes to you in thirteen chapters, each suitable for study for a weekly session across a three-month period. Study guidance, including possible goals, discussion questions, and learning activities, appears at the end of each chapter. The course may be covered in a briefer time span by lengthening class sessions or by combining chapters. One way to combine chapters is as follows: Session 1 (Chapters 1 and 2); Session 2 (Chapters 3 and 4); Session 3 (Chapters 5-8); Session 4 (Chapters 9 and 10); Session 5 (Chapters 11-13). Those desiring additional leader's helps for this course may find these in the September, October, and November, 1974, issues of *Christian Leadership* (Board of Christian Education, Box 2458, Anderson, Ind. 46011).

Key to Evangelism

1. <u>Simplicity</u> none of my prejudices

2. Roman Rd.

Romans 3: 23

4: 23   wages of sin is death

5: 8   yet sinners Christ died

10: 9 - Confess with one mouth

CONTENTS

Dedicated to my father
and to the memory of my mother.

Facing Up to Love

IT WAS AN OBVIOUS case of suicide: an elderly widow found dead in her apartment. On the table beside her bed was a diary. The final entry read simply, "No one called again today." Perhaps leaving that message was her last attempt to communicate with a world that had apparently failed to communicate with her.

"No one called again today." Reason for taking one's own life? Only those who have experienced the torment of loneliness are qualified to answer. This death would call for no coroner's inquest. There would be no manhunt for a ruthless killer. Still, we wonder if there was not a murder here. Was not this fragile soul killed by neglect? Who did this to her? Whose call was it that she had been expecting? Jesus expressly commanded, "Thou shalt love thy neighbor as thyself" (Matt. 22:39). But whose neighbor was she? No doubt everyone assumed she was being cared for by someone else.

Three Basic Attitudes

That's our presumed problem, isn't it? To know when we are responsible. But since when have we looked to an organizational chart to determine how we feel about people? Of the three basic attitudes we are capable of having toward others, one will be pre-eminent in each association, and it won't necessarily

7

be because we've figured it out that that's the way it should be.

Haters by Nature

We can hate people. No one assumes responsibility for hating another person. It is usually done spontaneously. It takes no self-discipline or specialized training. A person yields to the urge.

When Jack Ruby allegedly shot Lee Harvey Oswald, he may have felt he was acting on behalf of society and was executing justice. However, when Ruby first heard the news of President Kennedy's assassination, it is highly unlikely that he said to himself, "I ought to hate Oswald," and then proceeded to work up his anger. His hatred was likely instantaneous and unnurtured. Unless you believe in a sinister plot, responsibility had nothing to do with it.

Only God knows how many of us are basically haters. Though our hatred may not breed violence, it is possible that we bear in our hearts the same seething resentment—different only in degree, not in kind—that produces murder. This hate may be more common in society than anyone realizes, since most of us are sufficiently civilized to keep it largely bottled up inside us.

Hatred Will Come Out

Still the hatred in us seeps out like perspiration. The spirit of man has its pores, too. And so we catch ourselves feeling resentful of this one or that one. Could it be that the fever of hate rages deep down inside us? Is it not incidental which associate annoys us? Is

8

not the more relevant and alarming fact that inner hostility has keyed us to conflict even before the associate acts with impropriety? Hatred is a quarrel looking for a place to happen.

One day I walked into a hospital room in the maternity ward to be greeted by one of the most vengeful pair of eyes I've ever met. They belonged not to the patient, but to her guest, slouched as he was in a chair at the foot of her bed. Presuming him to be the husband of the expectant mother, I smiled and cordially introduced myself. He neither moved a muscle nor spoke a word. He just continued to glare at me in undisguised contempt. Awkwardly, the patient explained that she and the visitor were not married. I suspect he hated her and their yet unborn child would enter that man's world as I entered that room—hated before I arrived.

Hostility is not always expressed through violence or verbal abuse. Among the more cultured and religious it often comes out as snide criticism, backbiting, ridicule, impatience, gossip, negativism, and other devious devices.

The Source of Hatred

However varied its objects and expressions, hatred is usually traceable to a single (or at least, primary) source. The person who is generally contentious or sour is reacting to an experience—past or present—which has colored his entire outlook on life. During the course of a counseling session it became apparent to me that a young minister was saturated with hostility. Over the course of two or three meetings it emerged that he was angry at his congregation for not paying him a better salary, at his fellow ministers for not ordaining him, and at church headquarters for fostering so much worldliness. This led me to ask, "What are you *really* mad about?" Together, we discovered that he was carrying a chip on his shoulder which dated back to his boyhood days. He grew up hating the world because he had never taken revenge on his despotic father. Now, everyone else had to pay.

And so, we can hate people. This is certainly not the Christian norm, but it is one option available to us.

Indifference Is Another Possibility

We also have the alternative of being indifferent to people. One certainly need not assume responsibility for being indifferent. By definition indifference is akin to irresponsibility.

A young lady finally wrangled a date from a handsome fellow whom she had wanted very much to go out with. The next day her best girl friend, filled with curiosity, asked, "How did your evening go?" "I had to slap him three times," was the response. "That fresh was he?" exclaimed the friend. "No," answered the girl, "I had to do it to keep him awake."

Who has been trying to gain your attention? If he has succeeded, has it been worth his effort or has your interest been disappointingly dull? Recently, I visited the kindergarten department of our Sunday school. A doll-like little girl brought a pussy willow branch to show me. I knelt to be at eye-level with her. Quickly, we were joined by a second girl, equally lovely, who took advantage of my position to climb upon my knee. It was as if she were saying: Look at me; I'm important too. And so I divided my time between the two of them before rising to speak to other members of the class.

Neglect Is Dehumanizing

Neglect is a dull-edged knife. No one reacts kindly to being whittled with it. If a person suffers repeatedly from neglect, in time he will be reduced to a splinter. Splinters are sharp and someone usually gets jabbed. But the person jabbed by this splinter will probably not get the point. Instead, he will more than likely ask, "What's he so angry about?"

Indifference is like silence. But it is not eloquent; it is profane. It is like a curse, minus the vocabulary. If the recipient of our neglect suspicions his unacceptability, our silence confirms it. No one is overlooked without being made to feel shorter.

In the midst of a hotly contested local election campaign, a business man once said to me, "There has only been one office holder that I really did not want to see reelected." Then he told me this story. He had been stationed in France at the close of World War I. President Woodrow Wilson came to France to participate in working out terms of the peace. While there he was called upon to give a speech. A great crowd was assembled. The President addressed the French in their own language. "But," reported this man, "he never said a single word to his own troops who were there. There were American soldiers there who were sick, those who were in wheel chairs and on crutches, most

11

of them seeing their president for the first time, and he did not so much as acknowledge their presence." With harshness in his voice, the storyteller concluded, "I never had much use for Woodrow Wilson after that." Though you will have to determine for yourself the merit of the story, it illustrates the impact which neglect is capable of making.

Indifference May Be Carnal

Indifference may be hatred on good behavior. It is often a passive expression of anger—an attempt psychologically to blot out those toward whom resentment is felt. Clinically speaking, indifference is considered antisocial if adopted as a life-style. In other words, it is symptomatic of the beginning stages of mental illness. It expresses an unhealthy wish to live in isolation. To live aloof from society is a judgment upon either self or society, a declaration that one or the other is not okay. At very least, indifference toward others betrays self preoccupation and insecurity. It is an indication that one's life is bounded by his own concerns.

And so, we can be indifferent to people. Though perhaps not as un-Christian as anger, it is certainly sub-Christian.

Love Is the Highest Choice

We come, then, to the third alternative available to us: We can love people. Nothing less is acceptable to Christ. Here is the norm he left us: "Thou shalt love thy neighbor as thyself."

The parable of the good Samaritan teaches that

our neighbor is anyone who needs us. The lesson leaves no place for passing the buck. With love, as with hate and indifference, the question of legalistic obligation is completely irrelevant. Responsibility goes with awareness, and it's our business to be aware! Christ's approach to mission goes like this: Give a man a loving nature and then let him do what comes naturally. Love helps as spontaneously as hate hurts. Love notices while indifference nods.

Each of us has a gift of love to express. The more we open ourselves to God and his love and the more we express that love, the more love we have to share. Love is a gift that is given to us. It is something that we can grow in the life of every person. It is something that can be expressed by everyone, from the youngest to the oldest, from the most humble to the most famous, from the least schooled to the most highly educated. But to grow and flourish, love needs to be expressed. If it is suppressed and ignored, it withers.

Blessed be that community of persons who are tied together by bonds of Christian love. The church in which love toward each other and toward the needy persons of the world and toward God is expressed is a church that will flourish.

It Is Our Responsibility to Love

As Christians, we should need no coaching along the Jericho Road. The gaping wounds of humanity are simply not going to be healed by those who limit their sense of responsibility to family and friends. As sure as we parcel out the world that way someone will be left out; like the Greek widows of the early church. If healing is to come it will come through those who cultivate Christ's capacity to hear cries no one else hears and sight tears no one else sees.

Love is the genius as well as the genesis of ministry. It not only prompts us to serve; it enlightens us as to how best to do it. Love always finds a way.

A friend of mine who was enrolled in a class taught by Dr. Wayne Oates, distinguished professor at Southern Baptist Seminary, told me that Dr. Oates spoke at an orphanage down-state in Kentucky. Having been raised in poverty he told the boys and girls how he used to make his own toys when he was a child. Returning to Louisville, he learned that a new book had just been published on how to make toys at home using common household items. Dr. Oates bought five copies of the book and sent them to the orphanage. Those who know this great man well say that this is typical of Dr. Oates' thoughtfulness of others in unstructured ways.

Love Is Impulsive in Service

Compassion is compulsive. Those who are controlled by love are inclined to be uncontrolled in their sacrifice. Judas condemned the woman who emptied her alabaster jar of ointment upon Jesus in adoration. He protested that money from the sale of this might have been used for the poor. Yet, do you ever read of Judas doing anything for the poor? Evidence points to the fact that Judas had no charity but Judas. He wanted to argue responsibility. He sounded pious, but it was the impetuous woman who was the doer. Love comes through in season and out. Jesus said, "She has

14

done a beautiful thing." Love doesn't deliberate, "Who is my neighbor?" Love declares, "Such as I have I give." Love is made perfect in its impulsiveness. Legalists know nothing about this.

I worked my way through college and seminary largely through summer employment. The summer before my senior seminary year jobs were scarce. I searched for work in Michigan, then Indiana, and finally Ohio. A Middletown construction firm hired me to shovel pea gravel around foundations. Until I was able to secure lodging I made my home with a dear couple who provided me room and board without cost. Their daughter and my fianceé were special friends, but they scarcely knew me. I was hardly any responsibility of theirs. Still, they treated me as a son. "Pop" Lucas has gone to be with the Lord now, but I'll always remember him as an example of a caring person. Just thinking about him makes me face up to love.

HELPS FOR STUDY

Goals

To understand that we can take basic attitudes ranging from hate, through indifference, to love for persons around us.

To begin an exploration of what love calls us to do as Christians serving through the church and living in fellowship with each other.

Questions to Discuss

1. Are there times when indifference can be as bad or worse than hate?
2. Why do people sometimes say it is as bad to hate a per-

son as to commit murder? *When you hate—Pg. 8*

3. In what sense is indifference to other people going against God's will? *God said love.*

4. How many different meanings of "love" can you think of? In what way is love always alike? What is different about Christian love?

5. In what sense can a person change his basic attitudes himself? How does God help? *Someone always there to help.*

Learning Activities

1. Build definitions of key words from this chapter in the style of "Happiness is a warm puppy." Only you will use, "Hate is . . . ," "Indifference is . . . ," and "Love is . . ." (Eg., "Hate is a stone in your shoe." "Indifference is doing the dishes in cold water.")

2. Look through the newspapers, magazines, and family photo albums, noting whether each person you see there stirs some reaction ranging from hate through indifference to love. How strong is the feeling? Be honest with yourself? Why do you have the feeling? What all is involved in your love feelings? Do you feel indifferent to too many? Why or why not?

3. Share with one or two others whom you feel close to. What are some of your basic attitudes? How can they be changed?

"Love Is Our Style"

MANY YEARS AGO when Japan and China were locked in armed conflict, a Japanese soldier came to worship at a Chinese Christian church. The Chinese considered the Japanese territorial aggressors, and the presence of this enemy soldier in the service stirred considerable consternation. Perhaps sensing the alarm he had caused, the soldier stood to his feet and announced, "I am a conscript soldier; but I am a Christian. I would worship with you this morning." With that he became at once welcome. Following the worship service, the strange guest asked the pastor of the church to sign his name in his Bible, a Bible he had brought from Japan. To his signature the Chinese host added, "In Christ there is neither Jew nor Greek."

Love Transcends All Barriers

The church is the one place in all the world where love should overcome every barrier. The Apostle Paul could have identified readily with that Japanese soldier, for he too had known what it was to be thought of as "an enemy in the camp." As a new believer Paul sought to join himself to the community of believers who were met for worship at Jerusalem. They were all afraid of him until Barnabas vouched for him, telling the believers about Paul's mighty preaching in Damascus following his conversion.

To tell another believer that you are a Christian

17

should be sufficient information to assure him that he has found a friend, yes, even a brother. That statement must never suffer amendment nor conditional clauses. It is either true as it stands or the Church of Jesus Christ is violated. Perfect love provides perfect unity. Not necessarily universal agreement about doctrine or procedure. Not necessarily uniformity of standards or practices; but "unity of the Spirit in the bond of peace."

Love Results from Salvation

The moment "the love of God is shed abroad in our hearts" through the experience of salvation we are equipped to be the most unique community on earth— an unbroken circle of love. Those who belong to the church are mandated to "love one another" because it is to be our nature to do so. No human organization (to the best of my knowledge) requires members to love one another on grounds that a miraculous transformation has taken place in their hearts. Only the church makes such extravagant claims. The church even dares to make love the test of membership. John writes, "We know that we have passed from death unto life, because we love the brethren" (1 John 3:14). Of course, this is no more stringent than the test Jesus made for discipleship, "By this shall all men know that ye are my disciples, if ye have love one to another" (John 13:35).

You see, love is not just *ideological* with the church. It is also very *theological*. It is not just a noble aspiration we strive toward for the betterment of society. It is an expression of the regenerating power of Chris-

18

tian conversion. It is here more than anywhere else that our claims to new life in Christ must prove themselves true. Either the saints love one another or their salvation is worth no more than the buttons on their lapels. Either Christ knits us together by the cross, or the cross is no better a needle than education, social reform, and all of the other tools which men have employed in vain to "bring us together." Love has to win in the church because it is "our thing." If we can't make it work, who can?

Love Is the Life of the Church

Brotherhood is derived from a spiritual quality of life. It belongs only to the sons of God. It is one redeemed soul fellowshiping another redeemed soul in recognition of their common possession by Christ. In a study paper prepared for a Consultation on Doctrine this author wrote, "The church was not only *essential;* it was *inevitable.* It is the natural result of the kinship felt between twice-born men. The relationship of the body to the head defines the relationship of the members of the body to each other. To paraphrase an old theorom of geometry, 'Things equal to the same thing are equal to each other.' Accordingly, Christ, '. . . having made peace through the blood of his cross, (did) reconcile all things unto himself . . . ' (Col. 1:20) and to each other. Our peace with God polarizes the church around the son."

Those in the church do not just *happen* to love one another. They love one another because "love is of God," and *they* are of God. As sure as fish swim and birds fly Christians love one another. This fact

19

was a great mystery to those who were first confronted by the church. The church burst out of the Upper Room into a world of perhaps unprecedented hate and suspicion. The heavy heel of Roman oppression galled men into malice not only toward the emperor, but even toward their neighbors. Hurling an oath at one's stubborn ox seemed to release a little of the pent-up anger. Toppling a street vender's errant wagon was the next best thing to over-throwing the empire. Stoning a condemned harlot was a catharsis for self-hate.

Then a new breed of men appeared on the scene: men who gave a soft answer that turned away wrath. Men who not only did not curse the ox who had fallen in the ditch, but who helped him out, even on the sabbath. They blessed and cursed not. When they came upon those who had been vandalized by the roadside they did not sneer and pass by on the other side. They stopped to give aid. They forgave their enemies and did good to those who despitefully used them. They rendered unto Caesar without complaint and were subject unto the civil authorities. Even those who were slaves willingly obeyed their masters, and masters loved their slaves. Most obvious of all was how these unusual people seemed to live for each other. "Behold how they love one another," outsiders exclaimed. Such was the witness of the first century church to the world.

Love Covers a Multitude of Divisions

I have seen that New Testament Church reproduced in places where I have pastored. I cannot speak too

20

glowingly of those wonderful people who were closer than any human family, and yet were always open to welcome new members into the family. I have seen board members rise above differences of opinion and never speak aught against one another. I have seen misunderstandings transcended by love that was greater than pride. I have seen forbearance that survived personality idiosyncrasies. I have seen doctrinal differences discussed with candor and then laid aside without malice. I look back at the times I was not wise enough or big enough to keep God's people together. Yet, they stayed together. "Behold how they loved one another" is the best explanation I can give.

Unity Must Be Spiritual

We are destined to failure if we seek to create unity in the local church between any other than the born-again. Men and women cannot relate to one another as Christians unless they *are* Christians. Love cannot be practical until it is experiential. It is all but impossible to love as a matter of self-discipline. Koinonia is not achieved by the will of the flesh. It is the gift of the Spirit. Organization is never a sufficient foundation upon which to build the church. We have settled for affiliation when the church was made for fellowship. Joining the unregenerate to a local congregation is a vain exercise. At best it will produce indifference among the members toward one another. At worst it will produce division. That congregation of people composed of both saved and unsaved is not "fitly framed together"—Ephesians 2:21. It is not a "holy temple in the Lord." It is not Christ's way of construc-

21

tion. It is a hodgepodge of old and new lumber. He said, "I will build my church and the gates of hell shall not prevail against it." And how did he do it? By "adding to the church daily such as should be saved" (Acts 2:47). Were any but the saved added to the church, a little of hell would have gone into the church, and like the Trojan horse, would foster its overthrow. The church which endures is that one made up of "lively stones . . . built up a spiritual house, an holy priesthood, to offer up spiritual sacrifices, acceptable to God by Jesus Christ" (1 Peter 2:5).

Division Degrades Christ

Local division, even more than denominational division, is a scandal upon the name of Jesus Christ and the heartbreak of those caught up in it. A fine young man in one of the congregations I served flew to a southern state to participate in arrangements for a business convention. That evening in the motel, he stretched out on the bed to do some reading before falling asleep. He had taken along a copy of *Be-Attitudes for the Church,* just off the press. His roommate was curious and inquired, "What are you reading?" That book has a great deal to say about the dynamics of local church unity. Bill's roommate that night was an active layman in a prominent denomination. When he learned the nature of the book, he shared with Bill his great heaviness even at that hour because of the friction which was tearing apart the congregation to which he belonged back in Indianapolis. It seems reasonable to wonder how many members of that congregation were unconverted, basically carnally minded men who had "joined the church" out of a desire for prestige, fellowship, fear or guilt, or perhaps altruism.

Love Dares Not Be Superficial

To be perfectly honest, however, we must admit that evangelical congregations, too, have had their share of strife. Just because a person has made his way to the altar does not necessarily mean that he has been possessed of love. Some of us have written love on our Sunday cuffs so that we can give the right answer in church. However we have not learned love as a way of life. Consequently, when we are caught off guard without time to peek at our sleeves, we give an entirely different and altogether wrong answer. The test of our character is seldom announced in advance. So indelibly learn that love is the answer that it will be an automatic response in every trying relationship.

We may as well face it that we are not ready to proclaim the love of Christ to the world until we have first practiced it among ourselves. For a number of reasons (some of which will be discussed in succeeding chapters) we do not always possess the perfect love essential to perfect unity.

Love Heals Our Differences

Nearly twenty years ago a friend of mine became pastor of a congregation that was, according to him, divided three ways. For several months he struggled unsuccessfully to overcome the dissension. He wanted to have a series of revival meetings but because of the situation there was no money to pay an evangelist. Finally he determined to do the preaching himself.

Attendance had dwindled so drastically that it was decided to hold the services in the chapel rather than in the main sanctuary. Midway through the week the pastor felt he could carry the load no longer. During the invitation he said something close to this: "You people know the mess our church is in. If we can't get it straightened out we might as well close the doors. I want you to bow your heads and listen to me. If you are willing to forgive everything that has happened in this church in the past no matter how wrong you consider anyone else to have been, kneel there at your pew and pray." One by one folks got down on their knees. Finally only three couples remained seated. One of those knelt together. The second went down side by side. For what seemed like an eternity the third couple refused to budge. The pastor waited and wondered what to do next. At last the third couple knelt. The pastor then began to pray. He says that the Spirit came upon him in a mighty way. All over the audience, tears began to flow. When he had finished praying men who had not spoken to one another in over a year arose and embraced one another. My friend says, "From that day this congregation began to go forward." Today it is one of the finest churches among us. The pastor took me to that chapel and pointed to the very pew where twenty years ago the last couple had knelt to pray. He encouraged me to tell this story as an encouragement to others to take the way of love.

HELPS FOR STUDY

Goals

To take steps in making the way of love our way of living.

To grow in understanding the implications of love for the way the church fellowship is carried out and for the way it fosters unity.

Questions to Discuss

1. "Love transcends all barriers," says the text. Even though you basically agree with that, does it seem to you that there are some barriers that should be maintained? If so, what kind? *Physical love!* *Yes*

2. While love is described here as coming from salvation, what about all those people who lay claim to salvation but don't show much love? *They haven't realized that love grows w/ salvation*

3. What is the meaning of the idea that unity must be spiritual? How do mergers, practical cooperation between church bodies, and everyday Christian fellowship fit in?

4. Why is division sinful? It is sometimes argued that we need different kinds of churches to serve different kinds of people. It is sometimes said that there are often more differences between persons in a given church body than between them and certain Christians in other groups.

5. What is there about love that heals our differences?

Learning Activities

1. List all the kinds of barriers you can think of that come between persons. Then take some of the most important ones and consider how love changes things on both sides of the barrier and in the barrier itself.

2. Write, tape, or just think through a description of a person who has the highest kind of love as his life-style. Share and compare this description with others who have done the same thing.

3. Make a study of your community. What are the chief barriers that arise among its people? Among the church groups here? Consider how these barriers might be broken.

Somebody In There Likes Me

THE FELLOWSHIP of the church must be inclusive—not exclusive. Love that is sectarian is contradictory. The image of the church we see described in Acts 2 is that of an open fellowship. "And all that believed were together . . . and they, continuing daily with one accord in the temple, and breaking bread from house to house, did eat their meal with gladness and singleness of heart" (Acts 2:44, 46).

Recognition for Everyone

A popular syndicated columnist often reminds his readers that each of us wears a button on his chest which says: I want to feel important. The church ought to be a place where indeed *everyone* feels important: the widow who has but a mite to give, the little child to whom Christ has likened the kingdom, the woman whose reputation was not what it should have been before Jesus saved her, the rich like Lydia, the lettered like Nicodemus, the ignorant and unlearned like Peter, the disinherited like the lepers. Everyone!

Not that the church has nothing better to do than spend its time inflating egos. This is exactly what it attempts when it becomes an elite social club—whether composed of the ultra rich or the ultra spiritual. Nor are we very helpful when even in all sincerity we "bend over backwards to be nice" to someone who has two strikes against him. God commands us to give special attention to his "little ones," but may he save us from our patronizing, condescending attitudes toward those whom we receive more as a Christian duty than as a free expression of love. How sickening to be "made over" just because you are black, poor, handicapped, "new," or whatever. Let us love, but let us be authentic in our expressions.

Paul says, "For he [Christ] . . . hath broken down the middle wall of partition between us" (Eph. 2:14). That should have been the end of exclusivism in the church—but barriers still exist in many local congregations. For the most part the persons who have erected those barriers are oblivious to them. They don't realize what they have done. They are not intentionally shunning anyone. It's just that having eyes to see they do not see the lonely individual who looks longingly upon their good times and wishes he were included. It's just that having ears to hear they do not hear his hints that he too has a contribution to make or a need to be shared. There are too many outside insiders in the church.

We do not need to make anyone *feel* important. *also means at work* Everyone *is* important. If we would awaken to that fact we would overlook none. We would belittle none. If anyone is a member of the church he is one ransomed by Christ's death. If Christ died for him, how important is he? Sometimes our practice lags far behind our theology.

27

Is Everyone Really Welcome?

It is perhaps fair to say that most congregations are dotted with pockets of isolation in the midst of communities of love. It seems good when a church says it loves everybody, unless, that is, you happen to be an exception to the rule. When I was a boy it was common for churches to put on their outdoor signs, "Everyone Welcome." I venture to say that more than one person's experience has been such as to make him want to spit on signs like that.

After I had conducted the funeral of his little boy, a certain man told me that he didn't go to church much. And then he gave me a reason that on the surface didn't seem to make much sense. He said, "I don't think people ought to make fun of a child's shoes when he goes to church." In that moment I saw a small boy twenty years before marching off excitedly to Sunday school, and then coming home torn apart inwardly by the discovery that he was not accepted because his shoes were worn out. Maybe my imagination got the better of me. I hope so.

Apathy Appears as Coldness

But it isn't only those we treat disrespectfully that we lose. The apathy of fine Christian people probably drives away more persons than do the unkindnesses of the relatively few.

While attending a conference on evangelism I found myself seated at dinner next to a pleasant, unassuming young public school teacher. She impressed me as being an enthusiastic and committed Christian. This prompted me to inquire about her church life as a college student only a few years earlier. Happily, I learned that she had been active in church during college days, continuing a practice begun while still a child at home. She appreciated the church's ministry to her while away at college but found that one congregation excelled in this over another. She had changed church homes during her sophomore year in search of warmer friendships. What one congregation had lacked she found in another.

The local church must share its love if it is to be known as a community of Christ and enjoy the support of those looking for meaningful inclusion in the fellowship. What less could be asked of us? If the saints are not faithful over a stranger's visits they will never be made rulers over his will to return. Fellowship, too, has its stewardship.

Bacon said, "A crowd is not company, and faces are but a gallery of pictures, and talk is a tinkling symbol where there is no love." Let the church ponder that.

Friendliness Is Our Plus

The person on the edge of the church must often feel like a shopper who hasn't received his trading stamps as promised. He comes to our worship services where he fills his cart with singing, preaching, and announcements. He puts his money (much or little) in the collection plate and checks out following the benediction. At that point he begins to look for that little something extra which gives this congregation an edge over the one down the street (the "merchandise"

29

in his cart may not be superior to what he might have gotten elsewhere). Before he departs the premises he wants to know, "But where are the trading stamps I was promised?" In other words, "Where is the special love I was to receive for having come here?" If you want him to come back, church, don't forget the "trading stamps."

One man who had been quite a "rounder" prior to his conversion forsook his former haunts and departed from his former friends. He took his place among people of the church and took them to be his new friends and source of companionship. At first there was the customary "to do" made over him. Then, everyone just seemed to drop him. Patiently the man waited for members of the church really to accept him. Sunday after Sunday he suffered through the perfunctory handshakes and expressionless greetings. Remembering the good old days when he was never without cronies, he did a very level-headed things. He went to the pastor of the church and said, "Pastor, I'm suffocating for want of friendship."

If there is a newcomer to your congregation, go out of your way to get acquainted with him. Invite him into your home for a meal or snack. Find out when his birthday is and send him a card. Do more than scrawl your hurried signature. Take a few minutes to write a couple of lines that are warm and personal.

Love Is Not Reserved for Special Friends

Because we follow the line of least resistance in love, Christians gravitate toward one another. This, of course, has an advantage since it affords sustaining strength. Unfortunately, however, it also has a serious disadvantage. By surrounding ourselves with the loving, we insulate ourselves from those who most need our love. Thoughtless love is always exclusive.

Living in our beautiful world of lovely people we find it easy to applaud ourselves for "loving everybody." And we do! If, that is, the "everybody" is understood as meaning all those with whom we deliberately choose to associate and not literally the "everybody" out there beyond the walls of our little clique.

I remember how excited a minister's wife once sounded when I phoned unexpectedly. Her husband was a fine person and fairly prominent. It was apparent she did not know who was calling. She obviously assumed I was a dignitary from "headquarters," or perhaps an illustrious preacher or gospel singer. What a disappointment to learn who I really was. Her voice trailed off like one on a record when the stereo is suddenly unplugged. Love me? Yes, if I was the right person. Otherwise, no. That kind of selectivity has no place in the church.

Lofton Hudson writes, "The trouble with our love is that it is not love at all; it is a shrewd business deal: 'I will love you, if you will love me, or show appreciation, or in some way feed my ego.' "*

Love Takes the Initiative

Our love must become more aggressive. We must

---

*Lofton Hudson, *Helping Each Other Be Human* (Waco, Texas: Word Books, 1970), p. 53.

take the offensive in initiating love. As Christians the burden of proof is on us to instigate fellowship. We shall have to learn to reach out to others (even when our temperament inclines toward shyness). John tells us that it is a characteristic of God to love others into loving him (1 John 4:19). This is a side of our personality that most of us need to develop.

For four years I walked across college campuses "saluting" those who saluted me. For three more years I walked across a seminary campus doing the same thing. Then several years later I did some graduate work and painfully discovered that love asks more than I had realized. I despised myself for the years I had loved only those who loved me. What a cheap way to lay claim to fellowship.

Nothing will constrain a newcomer to become active in the life of the congregation more than being treated like a first-class citizen. If he can drive up to the church building and say to himself, "Somebody in there likes me," he will feel committed to that church. And more importantly, God will have hold of him. As he experiences the love of God through the fellowship of God's people his soul becomes welded to the soul of God.

It's been many years ago, but he still remembers it very well. He had never gone to church, didn't know anything about being a Christian and didn't really care much to know. But he was a whiz-bang of a softball pitcher and some fellows from the church asked him to come pitch for their team. Without giving it much thought he agreed. Of course, there was a hooker in the deal. In order to be eligible to play he had to attend worship several times a month. That's where the surprise came in. He soon found out that those church people cared about him. They loved him, not as a pitcher but as a person. The softball season ended but not his church going. He became a Christian and entered into numerous other activities of the congregation. To this day you'll find him there in church, right up front.

What About Those on the Inside?

Before we rush out to love the sinner beyond the doors of church, let us give thought to the unloved people right before us. Following World War II our nation was obsessed with helping the hungry of the world. It took us twenty years to notice the poor at home. The church has sometimes been like that. Just because we allow a man sixteen inches on a pew doesn't mean we've accepted him. He can be as lonely as a stranger on Times Square on New Year's eve. We must have a strategy for reaching the person who has made it through the door, but as yet, not into anyone's heart.

Jesus made it his special business to love the people no one else noticed. In fact, some of the New Testament's most distinguished citizens were outsiders until he took them in. The list includes Zacchaeus, Bartimaeus, Mary Magdalene, and others. Can you think of someone who needs your special attention?

33

Acts 2:44, 46 - pg. 26 - (someone read)
The Fellowship of the Church must be inclusive - not exclusive.

HELPS FOR STUDY

Goals

To practice sharing love through the fellowship of the church.

To learn more about how to draw people into the loving fellowship of the church.

Questions to Discuss

What is involved in helping

1. How can we make more people in our congregation realize their importance? - *Love ① - 5*

2. When someone appears cold and distant to you, how often is that really true of him? Or how often might it be shyness, preoccupation, or the way his face is built? What approaches do you take to the cold looking person?

3. You find friendliness both inside and outside the church. How is friendliness a special mark of the Christian? How is it a special mark of the church? - *8*

4. Who are some of the unloved people close around us? How can we recognize them? What do we do about it?

Learning Activities

1. Write some notes of loving appreciation to people you know who don't ordinarily get appreciated much.

2. Consider why you picked the people you did for the first activity and how you usually address them. Consider what all this says about the Christian fellowship.

3. Imagine what Zacchaeus, Bartimaeus, and Mary Magdalene would have to say about Jesus and his acceptance of them. You could role-play this as an interview between the person and a reporter.

→ our inconsistencies?

→ read no. 1 - then after comments - read no. 4 + ask for comments.. "What does love really ask of us?"

34

→ after no. 1 - how can you personally show attention to a person whom you see that needs help? How did Jesus show attention?

→ Begin w/ Pg. 26 - para. 1 to scripture -

Love
And Our Illusions

"WHAT SHALL WE SAY when they open the door?" The question was asked by a member of our congregation who along with a number of other persons was preparing to participate in a house-to-house Scripture distribution. Someone suggested, "Why not say, 'God loves you and I love you.' " Yet a third person objected to this, declaring, "There is no way I can tell a total stranger that I love him and say it with any degree of integrity."

Love Involves a Commitment

Let's not argue about whether a genuine concern to see everyone converted amounts to universal love. On those terms it should be possible to say to even a total stranger, "I love you." That's not the issue. The issue is just how authentic we are when we spew out sentiment in the name of religion on the shirt fronts of people to whom we have made no commitment and have no intention of doing so. "God loves you and I love you." That's fine and noble—nothing, in fact, can surpass it as pure Christianity—providing we really mean it. But if we don't, it's a watered-down imitation of the feeling Jesus had for the rich young ruler. It's an embarrassment to Christ and a lie to the world.

Is Our Love Fluctuating?

Our minds are so adept at playing tricks on us. Let us have a warm spot in our hearts for anyone and we think that's love. It happens not only with the stranger whom we hope to win to Christ. The same applies to anyone who tickles our fancy. Let a family member or fellow Christian do something that we approve of and our affection for him overflows its banks. Or let him say something complimentary of us or of someone we hold dear, and again we cannot contain our feelings about him. Or let him do us a special favor and see how quick we are to idolize him.

King Saul wanted a comely young man with sound character and a good heritage to entertain him. The engaging and handsome shepherd boy, David, son of Jesse, fit the order to a "T." David came to play his harp for Saul. The king liked the music because it soothed his troubled soul. He summoned David back for praise. David came and stood before Saul, and the scripture tells us that the king "loved him greatly" (1 Samuel 16:21). Yet, in but a short while Saul would hate David so intensely that he would try repeatedly to slay him. David had tickled Saul's fancy but when his effect on the king was adverse so were the king's feelings about him.

Love is not fleeting favor. If you can fall in love with someone who says your attire is becoming—you can fall out of love with him whenever his compliments turn to criticism. Any feeling that is conditional is therefore tenuous. And much of the good feeling we have for others *is* tenuous, as witnessed by the abruptness with which we become offended.

Love—An Action, Not Reaction

It is not difficult to love those who love us. Perhaps you and I cannot say as did one popular figure, "I never met a man I didn't like." But everyone of us can say: I never met a man who liked me that I didn't like. Ah, such a fellow: he is our kind of guy.

Now Jesus challenges us to assign greater responsibilities to love. He says, "Ye have heard that it hath been said, 'Thou shalt love thy neighbor, and hate thine enemy. But I say unto you, Love your enemies, bless them that curse you, do good to them that hate you, and pray for them that despitefully use you, and persecute you'" (Matt. 5:43-44). It is among the easiest things in the world to love those who love us, bless those who bless us and do good to those who do good unto us. It can also be a totally pagan practice. Such responses are not—whatever we have told ourselves—inherently Christian. Christ cautions us to expect no reward for this, asking, ". . . do not even the publicans do so?" (v. 47).

Love—More Than a Good Deed Now and Then

Another favorite trick of ours is to insist that we are loving persons because we are "so goodhearted." How that appeals to our vanity, to cite some good deed we have done and paint that as a true picture of ourselves! But the canvass of you and me is too big to be taken in by the swipe of a single incident, and if we face up

37

to it, we'll admit that not all of the strokes we make with the brush of daily deed are that becoming.

That marvelous Scottish writer, Alistair MacLean, writes, "I confess with the utmost frankness that the praise of good-hearted people leaves me cold. I have the smallest respect for them. . . . All the good-hearted people I have known are the creatures of pure emotion, and you can no more trust them in the matter of steady thinking and steady doing and steady giving than you can the weather. You know the type I mean. They give a couple pounds to a widow and forget her existence the rest of their lives. They spend ten shillings on a whim and on Sunday offer the God of heaven and earth a copper. They do one thing and proceed to salve their conscience with the idea they have done everything."*

MacLean may be a bit too hard on these people, for I have known many good-hearted people who were as steady as the sun at high noon. Still, he is right about the danger of letting our goodness be ruled by whim. We can't limit our love to the times the spirit moves us. There are days when the milk of human kindness doesn't rise in me. At such times love has to be a matter of discipline, a response to a commitment that knows no season and minds no tide.

Love Is Consistent

I remember a moving scene from a popular television series featuring a benevolent bachelor uncle, his two nieces and a nephew, and a very British butler. In one episode the children became objects of attention

---

*Alistaire MacLean, *Radiant Christianity* (London: Allenson & Co., 1942), p. 161.

of several young social crusaders who had a great deal to say about love. They sounded so right and seemed so superior to ordinary human beings. These impostors of love, however, soon defaulted on the obligations of love, floating away as quickly as they had come. Sobered by the disillusioning experience, one of the children said, "Uncle Bill is really the one who knows about love. He doesn't talk about it; but he took us in when we needed a home." Love is a fraud until it gets around to particulars: Whom? When? How? Where?

Love Gets Down to Cases

It is not too difficult to love the anonymous. Many of us have no doubt fancied ourselves at the side of Jesus sharing his compassion for Jerusalem as he looks down from the mountain upon the condemned city. As I listen to the daily news my heart aches for the whole world, and I, too, would like somehow to shelter it beneath the wings of my love. However, my nobility at times nearly faints when I meet that world face to face, "one to one." When it comes to living with them, the Herods and the Caiapheses aren't so easy to love as I had imagined.

Let us distinguish between loving from long range and loving close up. The former is much less demanding. We may love "sinners," but not Leroy Jones, local juvenile delinquent. We may love the Africans, but not the black family that has just moved into the neighborhood. We may love the "poor," but not that smelly little boy who rides the church bus to Sunday school. Great lovers—from a distance. Let's do better than that.

39

Love is nothing until it is expressed. Discount its genuineness if it abides only as silent sentiment or a noisy slogan while never taking the shape of deeds well done. The bus owned by one congregation bears the motto, "A Community of Christian Love." The inscription was recommended by a student who as an active participant in the life of the congregation was witnessing to the nature of the church as he perceived it. I believe that motto rings true because behind it stand thirteen task forces, manned by concerned Christian laymen and laywomen who perform the ministry of Jesus Christ seven days a week. And, of course, the nearly 300 people comprising those task forces are buttressed by a host of other persons whose service is unstructured.

Love is a great principle, providing it is applied to people, not theoretical situations. It is nothing in the abstract. It is everything in the concrete. If we cannot love those whom we have seen, how can we say we love those whom we have not seen? That's not Scripture, but it's pretty close.

It was said of one fellow that he loved everybody in general and hated everybody in particular. Check yourself. Love without a recipient is like a ship without a port. It sails the seas of fancied service with flags flying high. Yet it never unloads its precious cargo in any harbor of need or fellowships the misery of awaiting shoremen.

Meeting the Test

It was one of those hot summer days in the Ohio Valley when the sun seemed malicious in its attempt

40

to scorch all who dared venture out into its light. The afternoon seemed to linger deliberately as if to make sure everyone wearied in the heat. I left the comfort of my air-conditioned office to mail a letter in the box across the street.

While returning I saw an elderly man sitting on the steps leading to the church sanctuary. It was apparent that he was a transient, his entire belongings no doubt packed in the simple gym bag at his side. Many times travelers have come to my office seeking a handout. When they leave I wonder if the money I've given them will buy the meal they profess so desperately to need, or a bottle of whiskey somewhere down the road. I thought I might ignore this fellow. His head was bowed in semi-sleep. He had not bothered me yet; why should I invite a "touch"? Then I remembered the precepts set forth on these pages. I approached this traveler on our doorstep. Speaking softly so as not to shock him, I asked, "Are you all right?" Shocked none-the-less, he roused, focused his attention on me and replied, "Oh, yes, I have been hitch-hiking from Florida. I am sixty years old and I'm very tired." I invited him into the church to rest. He accepted with eagerness and appreciation. After "showing him to his room," I lingered to chat a little. With a decided New England accent he told me that he had once been a domestic of the late President John Kennedy. He recalled the day Mrs. Kennedy gave him $200.00 severance pay and a recommendation for a job in Florida. Now unemployed, he was returning northward, hoping to work a few more years to enhance his social security benefits. I left him there to sleep in the church nursery, an Irish Roman Catholic suspended in limbo between his past and his present. How do I know his story is true? I really don't, of course. But this I do know: Had I left him to wilt beneath the burning sun I would have no business writing a book about love.

HELPS FOR STUDY

Goals

To understand that the highest Christian love involves steady, committed action.

To arrive at a realistic view of Christian love apart from the romance sometimes associated with it or the disillusions about it.

Questions to Discuss

1. Is it possible for you to say and really mean it, "I love you," to hundreds of people? Why is this true or not true for you?

2. Most of our affection and good feelings toward other people goes up and down depending upon circumstances. The author says, however, that "love is not a fleeting favor." How, then, is true love different from our rising and falling affections?

3. "Love must get down to cases." What does this mean?

4. When people come asking for handouts, how should we respond? Should we always refer them to the correct welfare channels? Is it better to err on the side of generosity or caution?

Learning Activities

1. Study 1 Corinthians 13 to see how it undergirds this chapter. Make your own paraphrase of it or your own meditation guide.

2. What problems are people in your congregation and in your community having right now? Apply Christian love specifically to these cases. What does it say to these people? What does it say to you about them?

The Problem With Loving

TWO THINGS, it seems to me, most continually cause the children of God a sense of condemnation: their lack of faith and their lack of love. I say this having observed over a number of years the kind of preaching which moves congregations to repentance. This is also substantiated by what God's people say is bothering them when they come to me for counsel.

Now, I personally feel no community of men more richly abounds in faith and love than the church. I salute God's people for their remarkable levels of attainment at both points. Yet, the saints are basically correct in the assessment of their weaknesses and could not desire more wisely than they do. Indeed, it is my conviction that if a man were to possess perfect faith and perfect love, he could *be* perfect with no difficulty at all.

Love and Security

Significantly, lack of faith and lack of love both originate from the same source. Both are rooted in *insecurity*. The person who finds himself short on faith is unsure of what is his, whereas the individual who lacks love is unsure of who he is. The former is preoccupied with *having*, the latter with *being*. The two

43

fears often exist side by side since if one is basically insecure, he is vulnerable to threat at every point of meaning in his life.

Understanding the origin of our problem, it thus unfolds why we love some people more easily than others. Generally speaking, we love those who make us feel secure. Conversely, we dislike those who make us feel insecure.

It Is Easier to Love Those Like Ourselves

Let us be specific in applying the principles just listed.

We do not easily love those who differ from us. To say that opposites attract is only a partial truth. We may admire those whose strengths are our weaknesses and find complementary relationships with them (particularly if our strengths happen to be their weaknesses). Notwithstanding, it is unlikely that we will find a natural compatibility with those whose life-view contradicts our own at crucial points.

I remember as a child my first impressions of "not liking" certain people. There was the man across the street who worked as a bartender. There was the father of one of my friends who was a Roman Catholic. And there was the boy at school who poked fun at the presidential candidate of our family's choice. It was a strange and uncomfortable feeling not liking these people. Of course the animosity I felt toward them was largely unfounded. In each case our relationship was very limited. The single explanation for my resentment was that these three people represented segments of society quite different from my own

44

heritage. Each one of them in a different way represented a threat to several values which I had been taught to cherish.

The "We" and the "They"

We divide people into the "they" and the "we." As a result we love the "we" and hate the "they." Ironically, I have no childhood recollections of disliking any blacks. Again, the explanation appears quite simple. The blacks I knew were poor—just as I was. They were friends of our family. They belonged to the Church of God as we did and had the same moral convictions. They were "we" in many important respects. Hence, I liked them.

We invest our sense of self worth in such things as the race, creed, and color with which we are associated. However, that is far from an all-inclusive list. In some way or another we are one with many people and causes. We are prone to stigmatize those who find their identities in differing alignments. They may represent to us what the Greeks and the barbarians were to the Jews of Paul's day, presumed outsiders to the love of God. A partisan attitude about our own identity is a major source of prejudice.

Lacking a better reason for believing in ourselves, we may find those to look down upon in order to look up to ourselves. However, when we resort to such desperation tactics, we often do violence to the truth and face a difficult time when forced to be honest. Though sorely tempted, I never quite yielded to the silly notion that boys with long hair could not be as clean, decent, intelligent, and deeply religious as close-cropped fel-

45

lows. In time I grew a teen-ager who chose to wear his locks a little longer than mine. Hair-wise, the "they" became "we." Since fortunately in this instance I had no great prejudice toward the "they," it was no cataclysmic adjustment for me to accept my son's hairstyle.

Fear and Prejudice Hinder Ministry

If the church is to extend redemptive love to the world, those of us in the church must deal with our feelings toward the "they" people around us. We will never win them so long as fear and prejudice dominate our relationships with those different from us. What are our motives for wanting to make "we" people out of "they" people? Is it so they may have the same joy we possess (1 John 1:4)? Or is it to eliminate those who by their difference raise question marks about our position? Only as we can tolerate the nonconformity of others can we offer them the acceptance so essential to bridging the gap between us.

This same principle applies to relationships within the church. It is those insecure in their self-worth who frequently become storm centers in the local congregation. They bring on controversy by pushing for compliance, needing that conformity as evidence they are right, and needing to be right in order to feel important. Such were those in the early church who objected to anyone eating meat which had been offered to idols. Paul called them "weak in the faith" (Rom. 14:1) and abstained from the practice so as not to threaten them by his differentness. Someone has wisely said, "People who are riddled with doubts tend to be dogmatists who are never wrong."

Comparisons Influence Our Attitudes

We do not easily love those who surpass us. We may idolize a public official or sports hero and, by identification with him, emotionally share his success. However, we may not find much warmth in our hearts toward those of our peers with whom we are unfavorably compared, particularly if *they* foster the comparison.

We like the Joneses better if they don't get too far ahead of us. If Mr. Jones brings home a check approximating the size of that of our family's breadwinner, if Mrs. Jones doesn't out-dress our own Mrs. and if Junior Jones doesn't excel our boy in sports and academics, the Joneses will probably be fine people in our book. But if they begin to outdistance us; their faults may suddenly become very obvious to us.

What was the source of Cain's flaming hatred for Abel? Was it not that his brother—the one with whom he was habitually compared—had excelled him in an area of life very crucial to parental approval—namely religion. One fact sealed Abel's doom: God was pleased with Abel's sacrifice, but not with Cain's. Cain experienced humiliation. He did not elect to enlarge himself; but to destroy the measuring stick. Thus was the first murder committed.

Jealousy Comes from Feeling of Inferiority

Jealousy is but self-hatred turned outward. The jealous person concludes inwardly, "I am a failure."

47

Then he reasons, "But no one would notice if Joe were not such a success." Hence, Joe becomes the object of his resentment, when, in fact, his initial quarrel is with himself. He may not murder Joe, as in the case of Cain, but he may attempt measures (i.e., back-biting) aimed at cutting Joe down to his size.

There is an old Grecian story about a man whose jealousy led to his death. The man's fellow citizens had erected a statue to one of their number who was a champion in the public games. So intense was the jealousy of one of this hero's rivals, that every night after dark the man would go out to try to destroy the monument. After repeated attempts, one night he succeeded in dislodging the statue from its pedestal, whereupon it fell upon him and crushed him to death. In a sense, jealousy destroys all those who tamper with it.

We Are Not in Competition

Jealousy has no place in the fellowship of the church. Strife inevitably results when we vie for position, become competitive in performance, and treasure worldly status symbols more than the fruits of the spirit. It is a contented man who measures himself only by his own God-given potential in the light of his particular life situation and not by the achievements of others. Thus, he is threatened by no one else's successes. He strives only to be his best, content to know this is all life requires of him.

If we are sure of our own contributions (no matter how humble) we can rejoice in the contributions of others. We fear no loss of identity. When convinced that our own place in the hearts of those significant to us is secure, we gladly yield a place to others. Thus we are happy to win talented or affluent new people to Christ and rejoice to see established members excel in Christian service.

I marvel at the attitude of Jonathan toward David. Saul was extremely jealous of David, but not his son, Jonathan. David's great success apparently in no way strained his friendship with Jonathan. Throughout David's meteoric rise to fame and power, Jonathan remained loyal to David. We conclude that whereas Saul was unsure of his identity, Jonathan never doubted his own worth.

Our Twin Is a Threat

We do not easily love those whose weaknesses reflect our own. We may feel compassion toward those oppressed by sin or circumstances which we have overcome (or, on the other hand we may look down upon them in contempt since they are so much weaker than we), but we are not inclined to be charitable of those whose wretchedness typifies our own.

There is a great deal of fraternity among members of AA and much compassion on the part of AA people toward untreated alcoholics. This is understandable since AA members have accepted the reality of their problem and, hence, can accept others in the same predicament. However, listen to the comments of the alcoholic outside AA as a drunk passes by. Chances are the man who is temporarily sober will speak in derision of the man who is intoxicated. He sees him as a contemptible figure, more so than would the average citizen.

When surveying one whose ruin is unlike our own, we may say, "There but for the grace of God go I." We may get some satisfaction from that, but there is no satisfaction when the grace of God has not as yet been operative in our lives, and the fellow who moves before us compels an abbreviated observation, "There go I."

Projecting Our Guilt

What we condemn in others is often what condemns us. Because it exists in our own lives we are sensitized to observe it in the lives of others. It's like buying a green '70 Chevy hardtop and suddenly discovering that half the people in the world have one just like it. The reason David was so incensed by Nathan's story is that his conscience was already on the raw edge. He hated the man who had taken another's sheep because he had taken another's wife.

Beware of the person who is forever alerting you to gossips. He probably is one. Hold onto your pocketbook when you hear someone raving about the dearth of honest people these days. He doesn't trust himself and judges all others accordingly.

We Must Accept Others to Accept Ourselves

More objectivity among Christians about their own faults would create a much healthier attitude toward both fellow Christians and sinners. Having faced ourselves, it would not be so painful to see ourselves in others. Attacking our weaknesses directly would save

50

us from attacking them indirectly, as is the case when we condemn others self-righteously.

Having faced ourselves we must then take a positive attitude despite what we see. *The ability to have compassion for others rises from the ability to have compassion for oneself.* There is a distinction between compassion and self-pity. The former accepts; the latter excuses. The former is charitable, the latter is permissive. If we can forgive ourselves for being fallible, we can forgive others likewise. First, we must love ourselves in spite of ourselves. Then, we can love others in spite of themselves. If we rid ourselves of self-hatred, it is a lesser chore to rid ourselves of resentment toward others.

Jesus said to Peter, ". . . when thou are converted, strengthen thy brethren" (Luke 22:32). Peter did not qualify for that high calling by arriving at perfection. He qualified in due season as one who had heroically faced his own prejudice, pride, and failure. Out of his own experience of humanness Peter identified with the struggles of others—loving them as he had found Jesus to love him. Love can be ours only by the same formula.

Helps to Study

Goals

To face up to the difficulties in loving and find strength to love well.

To identify qualities that help us deal with barriers to Christian loving and to draw on helps.

Questions to Discuss

1. What are the two or three greatest barriers to expressing

Christian love?

2. What are the main qualities we can encourage in ourselves that help overcome the barriers?

3. "Jealousy comes from feelings of inferiority." Are there other causes? How can we deal with causes of jealousy?

4. If a person is basically fearful in his attitude toward life, what can be done to help him? What does the gospel offer here?

5. In what ways does an attitude of the "we" separated from the "they" creep into our lives? There is a degree of normality about it. How do we get around it?

Learning Activities

1. Get with a partner and talk about what makes it easy for you to like some people and dislike others. Consider ways around this barrier.

2. Expand on the following problem situations and then deal with ways of overcoming the barriers involved:

a. A husband and wife who have grown bitter and noncommunicative toward each other.

b. A Sunday school teacher and a child who constantly misbehaves and disrupts the class.

c. Two men in long and serious business competition.

d. A neighborhood where racial, social, and economic barriers have been raised.

Love Faces
A Trade Deficit

SOME YEARS AGO Geraldine Endsor wrote, "Love is the purification of the heart from self."

This helpful insight explains the magnanimity of love. Graciousness and nobility always co-exist with love for they flood the vacuum otherwise occupied by self. Love makes a person ten feet tall in character. He is a man at his best, always congenial, and generous to a fault.

Programmed for Self

If self were purified we could love others solely on the basis of their need, not on condition of a positive interaction of their lives with ours. Each of us has a computer within his psyche. Psychologists refer to this personality mechanism as our ego. You and I may think of it as pride or self. This computer is at work in every relationship. Unless programmed otherwise, it tends to sort out those persons who would serve our purposes from those who would not. Of the former it may say, "You may accept them; it is to your advantage." Of the latter, however, it may insist, "Reject them; they are hazardous." When self is purified, then, we are no longer so likely to make this distinction. *Love* becomes the computer. Our relationships are freed from inordinate concern, to further our own advantage.

Let us see specifically how the above principle works.

Vulnerable to Hurt

Acceptance is one of the primary yardsticks by which you and I measure our self worth. When we are loved or admired we feel reassured of our significance. We feel good about ourselves. However, rejection may cause us to doubt our significance. We feel it important to restore that lost confidence. We often do this by speaking or acting defensively.

The Apostle Paul experienced rejection from the church at Corinth. Certain members of the congregation did not respect his calling and ministry as he expected. They did not always abide by his teachings. He responded by vehemently defending his apostleship. But Paul had great insight into his own feelings—something lesser men lack. He said, "I have become a fool in glorying: (but) ye have compelled me: for I ought to have been commended of you . . ." (2 Cor. 12:11). Paul had invested himself in being a good pastor and came out looking like a poor one. That's very hard to bear, for even the most Christlike.

When others like us less, we feel compelled to like ourselves more. This is called compensation. The braggard is persuaded that he is not properly esteemed by others. Unfortunately, our exaggerated efforts seldom convince us. It is very difficult for us to think well of ourselves when others do not. No matter how invalid, we tend to acknowledge rejection as incriminating evidence.

Rejection is experienced in a variety of ways. None of us is a stranger to it. It is impossible to live in society and escape either criticism, disagreement, discrimination, ridicule, unfriendliness, slander, and other forms of rejection.

Hurt Makes Us Dangerous

The poorer one's image of self, the more vulnerable he is to feelings of rejection. Lacking confidence in his desirability, he will constantly test his acceptance, often in invalid ways which are sure to produce the illusion of rejection though none was intended. Not all relationships must be categorized. We are inclined to interpret nonacceptance as rejection, when in fact the feeling toward us may have been neither positive nor negative, but simply too slight to be other than neutral. Furthermore, not all associations must be 100 percent inclusive. Distance does not necessarily mean separation. Being occasionally left out does not necessarily mean rejection.

It is vitally important that we learn to handle our feelings of rejection. Left uncurbed, these feelings can cause us to act in destructive ways. As a youth Hitler wished to be a city planner. He used to walk around his hometown of Linz daydreaming. In his imagination he tore down large buildings and built new ones. One day he sent his plans for a new opera house to a prize committee which paid no attention to them. It was at that point Hitler broke with society. Crushed by this crowning rejection, he disappeared, only to reappear later as the most destructive force ever to strike the continent of Europe. Many factors made Hitler what he was, but rejection in a cherished field made a contribution to his twisted career.

We Must Find Acceptance

How can we put love in control of each experience of rejection so that we do not react in foolish or carnal ways? Here is a paradox: self is purged only when it is secure. *We can endure rejection from one source if we find acceptance from another, providing the latter source is at least as significant to us as the former.* As Christians we simply dare not allow our sense of well-being to be determined by how the world treats us. If we do, we'll be out of sorts much of the time. Support for our feelings of self worth must be based in relationships which are basically stable and fundamentally charitable.

Where to Find Acceptance

No one was ever more purged of self than Jesus. Where did he look for acceptance? To the world? No, he acknowledged that the world could hate him as readily as it could hail him. He even warned us that we would find this true also. Jesus depended upon his disciples for acceptance. It did not break his heart that Caiaphas should reject him, but there was deep feeling in the question addressed to Peter, "Will ye also go away?" Furthermore, Jesus drew great strength from God's acceptance of him. "I and the Father are one," he said.

How thankful we can be for the church wherein we

experience love that more than compensates for the ill-treatment heaped upon us by the world. I remember a young teen-ager who suffered great isolation in most areas of her life. Victimized by a broken home, her father lived in a distant state. Her mother, with whom she lived, worked long hours and seemed often pre-occupied with her own needs. Partially handicapped, she found few friends at school. The most meaningful relationships this young lady had were those within the church, particularly with members of the youth group and the church's minister of youth. That precious child of God has today an emerging sense of signifi-cance largely owing to the love which came to her through the Christian community.

How thankful we can be to our loving heavenly Father who through Jesus Christ has moved to express his acceptance of us in the pardon of sin. How can we ever feel threatened by the rejection of anyone when the Savior of the world has given his word, "I will never leave you nor forsake you"? When we moved to a new city our small son felt so very lonely on the school playground at recess, excluded from groups because he was a stranger. How much it meant to him to spend an hour in the evening playing with me, the one friend who remained. Even so, our heavenly Father is always the friend who remains.

Rejection Is Part of Life

Yet, we must expect those times when seemingly no one accepts us. We are not adequately prepared to cope with rejection until we have learned to accept ourselves no matter what the response of others to us. All but

57

one of the disciples did eventually forsake Jesus and flee. Even in the best of congregations misunderstandings occasionally occur. Even the most ideal fellowship can become strained. When this happens, we must reaffirm our self-worth. Thus strengthened, we will be able to admit our own part in the strife and to feel charitable toward those from whom we are momentarily estranged. Only as we properly love ourselves can we be objective about our relationships with others.

Furthermore, we may even find times when *God* seems to have rejected us. You remember Christ's mournful cry from the cross, "My God, my God, why hast thou forsaken me?" Never does a man need to believe in himself more than when the heavens seem to be made of brass and his prayers cannot penetrate them. At such times men less sure of themselves than Job reject God out of feelings of having been rejected by God. Men, however, who believe in themselves are able to "be still and know." They have the capacity born of inner poise to wait out the storm until God's faithfulness again becomes apparent.

Achievement Is Important to Us

Another yardstick by which we measure our significance is achievement. Our self-estimation is in part related to the goals we set in life and how successful we are in reaching them. Persons who assist us in the realization of our ambitions are easy to love. They contribute to our emotional security. However, the person who deliberately or incidentally hinders us in our pursuit of achievement may well be the subject of our resentment. He is not merely inconveniencing us.

58

He is preventing us from proving our significance. He frustrates us in our quest for fulfillment.

Paul had a burning ambition insofar as the church at Corinth was concerned. It was that believers arrive at a spiritual maturity. Repeatedly they disappointed him. It appeared at times they would always remain babes. Though in this case Paul's aims were far from selfish, this did not diminish his frustrations. Indeed, his zeal for the Lord's work being so great probably only served to intensify the frustration he felt. "Behold, the third time," he says impatiently, "I am ready to come to you" (2 Cor. 12:14).

Every day, situations arise in which you and I have vested interests. That is we stand to gain or to lose something by the outcome. There may be some stake which is more important to us than the actual cause itself or the issue being contested. Usually this secondary stake is our own pride. Under these conditions, the man who will further our objectives is thought of as a friend and the man who may impede our objectives is thought of as a foe. The divisiveness of this kind of thinking is obvious. Hence, so also as is the importance of purging selfish ambition.

Testing Our Motives

Because we are committed, most of us have strong feelings about "how the church should be run." This is good but it can get us into trouble. Others, equally committed and likewise Christian may have another opinion about how things should be done. Soon we may find that they are frustrating our ambitions by working counter to us—even if not maliciously. Before we allow ourselves to be drawn into conflict with these persons it is important for us to understand our own feelings. Why are we so adamant that it must be done our way? Is it because we are thoroughly convinced that is the best way to do it? Or, is it because we need it done that way in order to feel good about seeing our plan carried out? If the former reason applies, we will be able to concede, even though regretting that the results will perhaps suffer somewhat. If the latter reason applies, we will not be able to yield, not at least without smarting over the subsequent frustration we will inevitably feel as we remain unvalidated.

Sure of Ourselves

The person who is sure of himself will not find it difficult to respect the rights of others. As self is purged, defensiveness and willfullness diminish. We are less exposed to personal disappointment, less needy of success and prominence. There will be no favorites between those who like us and those who do not.

General Robert E. Lee was once asked his opinion of a certain man. General Lee replied, "He is a fine and able man." "But, General," protested the inquirer, "do you not know that he criticizes you and runs you down?" "Yes," answered Lee, "but you did not ask what he thinks of me. You asked what I think of him." Lee did not achieve the most crucial objective of his lifetime. Yet, he loved those who opposed him and accepted defeat with a sweet spirit. He was able to do this because he did not base his sense of well-being on winning the Civil War. That's important for us to remember in every conflict in which we are involved.

Perhaps few persons will frustrate our ambitions more than those whom we hope to win to Christ. If our purpose for evangelizing is to gratify our need to manipulate people or to appear as a great servant of God, we will be sore losers whenever our witness is disregarded. I recall the book salesman who insulted me when I would not buy his set of encyclopedias. It was obvious my purchase would have done him more good than me. If our desire to save others is pure we will experience sorrow rather than resentment when they turn aside. Looking for no reward, we will not be angry at gaining none.

Notice the beautiful way in which Paul expresses his commitment to love, at whatever cost to self. "I will very gladly spend and be spent for you; though the more abundantly I love you, the less I be loved" (2 Cor. 12:15). Paul faced his trade deficit without regret or misgivings.

Love Is Not on an Ego Trip

Love has higher priorities than self-promotion. Until an inordinate concern with self is swallowed up in a more comprehensive love, we cannot practice the Christian virtues of meekness and sacrifice. No one keeps books and does the ministry of reconciliation. Though men may reject us and thwart us; if through it all we can save some—that is most important. Gethsemane teaches us that even a Judas is not to be resisted if in affording him thirty pieces of silver he opens a door of redemption to us.

61

HELPS FOR STUDY

Goals

To gain in a sense of personal significance.

To find acceptance, to overcome hurts, and to overcome failure as a basis for showing forth Christian love.

Questions to Discuss

1. How common is it for people to feel overwhelmed by hurt, defeat, rejection?

2. Where can we best find healing, acceptance, and security within present-day society? beyond it?

3. What are the problems that go with a person being preoccupied with his own problems, the state of his ego, and the like?

4. In what sense is Christianity a religion that takes into account our psychological state? In what sense does it move far beyond that?

5. What is meant by "trade deficit" in this chapter?

Learning Activities

1. Think of someone you know who is or tends to be hurt, rejected, and defeated. How can you minister to this person? Lay out a strategy of loving ministry.

2. What's good about you? Make a list of your strong points. Build on that today. Remember, God loves you and regards you highly and dearly.

3. Get in a sharing group and tell each other what your strong points are.

also go into small groups for no. 2.

62

The Menace Within

Sept. 27

D̲R. LEON SAUL once said, "Within every grown-up lives the child he once was." Commenting on that, Lofton Hudson writes, ". . . This self-centered, I-want-my-way, why-doesn't-someone-love-me attitude is within everyone of us from the bassinet to the mortuary."*

Love Versus Childishness

It cannot be emphasized too strongly what a threat this child within you and me is to the love we hope to share. Our childish tendencies cause us to be spontaneous, playful, and at many points delightfully winsome. We would be dull and altogether bored if that side of our personalities were completely lacking (as seems to be nearly the case with some people). However, out of control, that child within us is a divisive, destructive force in every interpersonal relationship we might establish. This spoiled child poses as a friend, but, in fact, is a dire enemy. Not all of the friction which we experience with others can be laid to them. Some of it must be traced to the door of the child within us.

Paul said, "When I was a child, I spake as a child, I understood as a child, I thought as a child; but when I became a man, I put away childish things" (1 Cor. 13:11).

---

*Lofton Hudson, *Helping Each Other Be Human* (Waco, Texas; Word Books, 1970), p. 156.

At first glance we may wonder what this reference to childhood and manhood has to do with the subject of love, the dominating theme of the chapter from which the verse cited is taken. However, upon closer study we discover that what seems like an interjection, is, in fact, integral to the discussion.

The truth is that until childish things are put away love doesn't stand a chance. The child within us opposes each unselfish proposition of love. The war between these two is as ancient as that between God and mammon.

Competitors or Collaborators?

The child within us gets us into trouble because from the very start it takes an erroneous position. Typical of its misconceptions the child within us sees our associates more as competitors than collaborators. It is a childish persuasion that whatever one wants in life exists in limited supply and, therefore, he must get it first. And so, even our friends may be thought of as foes.

An entire nation watched in curiosity during the 1972 presidential primary to see what would become of the long-standing friendship between George McGovern and Hubert Humphrey as both vied for the nomination. One-time neighbors and colleagues in the senate, there had existed a warm relationship between them. As McGovern forged ahead in delegate strength, the pressure on Humphrey became intense to assail his opponent and to resort to tactics he had earlier disavowed. For stakes far less than the presidency of the

United States men have crucified their friends in order to further their own interests.

Selfish Ambition

The child within us burns with selfish ambition while seldom having a wise sense of value. Thus we can be unmercifully demanding even over trifles. With the child in control life becomes a daily duel with one contest following another. The world is experienced as a hostile environment. Society is a jungle where it is the survival of the fittest. The reason some people are so weary with life is that they have made it so competitive. They are always seeking to wrest wealth, status, or some other equally vain thing from life, usually at someone else's expense. Thus they live under constant pressure to "come out ahead." Little do they realize that the way of service would afford them much greater peace, as well as joy.

We may as well face up to it that love is not our style if we spend our days as greedy children at the candy counter. He who has become a man practices brotherhood, not rivalry. He views the world as a community and is persuaded that whatever he does for the common good works ultimately for his own good. Selfishness is too shortsighted a view for anyone claiming a mature understanding of life.

A reporter once asked a university football coach his system. "Well," replied the coach, "we use the color system. We just try to knock down anyone not wearing our color." That approach may work well on the football field but it is devastating as a philosophy of life. It is as alien to Christianity as Judas' blood money.

It is as out of place in the church as Caiaphas at the Last Supper. To the contrary, as disciples of Christ, our calling is to lift those who have been knocked down by the assorted vested interests in society which cut a swath through humanity attempting an end run.

Love Leads to Mutuality

Love's position is that whatever good fortune there is in life—whether it exists in abundance or scarce supply—should be shared. Love is social, not as a matter of politics but as a matter of passion. Quite a man was he—that boy who shared his five loaves and two fishes with the multitude. He had caught the vision Paul is calling for us all to embrace. Sharing brings us into community and opens new relationships to us. It may even produce reciprocity with gains we had never anticipated, though the latter is more a possibility than a promise.

During an important automobile race, a contestant stopped his car to pull a fellow driver out of the flaming wreckage of the latter's car. The delay cost the good Samaritan $7,500.00 in prize money. Brotherhood or rivalry? Again and again life compels us to make a choice and the choice we make is an index of our maturity.

Negativism May Be Childish

Typically, the child within us is temperamental, touchy, and tyrannical. One day while making pastoral rounds I stopped to see a woman at her place of business. It was really my first opportunity to get to know her. Customers were scarce that day (as I suspect they usually were) and so she talked freely (as I later learned she always did, whatever the circumstances). It was a tedious and disappointing visit. She lambasted everything and everyone we talked about except God, and how he escaped I'll never know. She had been in and out of the church for years, and yet few people respected her "brand" of Christianity. The resentment she showed for so many people betrayed a childish nature that was next to impossible to please. If one did not subscribe to her code of behavior, endorse her interpretations of the Scripture, indulge her prejudices, flatter her religious exercises, and celebrate her presence, he stood little chance of keeping her favor.

What irritates a man is a good indication of the kind of man he is. Jesus was angered that the money-changers had turned his Father's house into "a den of thieves." That was not pettiness. But it was pettiness that led Martha to complain to Jesus that her sister, Mary, was not helping with the household chores. Children wear their feelings on their sleeve; and it is pretty easy to tell where ours are when everyone has to watch his step so as not to offend us.

Maturity to Forbear

Let's be big enough to dismiss those trifling injuries that inevitably occur as the result of sharing fellowship in the body of Christ. Paul writes, "Put on then, as God's chosen ones, holy and beloved, compassion, kindness, lowliness, meekness, and patience, forbearing one another and, if one has a complaint against another, forgiving each other . . ." (Col. 3:12-13). As representatives of Jesus Christ we simply cannot allow the devilish child within us to destroy the fellowship and to disrupt the mission of the church. No man is ever going to be a blessing to others or an asset to God's cause until he "puts away childish things"—unequivocally and emphatically squelching his petty nature and siding with the better, more mature side of himself.

While still in seminary a friend and I served a small congregation some distance from the campus. There was in that congregation a gentle and committed woman who meant more to us than we were ever able to say. She was the church pianist but beyond that she was the person we could always look to when there was a job to be done. She was steady, loyal, and compatible. Almost every Sunday my friend and I were the guests of her and her husband for dinner. Because she accepted responsibility, she was at times the object of criticism from uninvolved persons in the congregation. Though this hurt her she never displayed the slightest trace of bitterness. Furthermore, she refused to play the martyr's role, yielding to self-pity. I learned early in my ministry to appreciate profoundly those hardy mums in the congregation who yield their flowers without special consideration, and even sometimes in spite of adverse conditions. I think God plants them especially for the pastors.

Servants or Companions?

Something else about the child within us: Consistent with his distorted view, associates are looked upon as servants, not companions. In childlike fashion many a person considers himself the center of the universe, with all that surrounds him existing but to serve his own wants and wishes.

We find this complex existing within families and among friends. Instead of living according to patterns of true companionship, some husbands expect their wives to be merely their household servants. Some wives expect their husbands to be their drudges, simply providing money, a house, transportation. Some children grow up with this same attitude toward their parents. One may take the same outlook toward friends. In so many ways we can reduce those around us to a status that makes them less than real persons, genuine companions, true friends. Love works in a different way in building up the fellowship of Christians and in extending their outreach into the world.

Thoughtlessness

The child within us is all but utterly thoughtless, caring not for the needs, feelings, or rights of others. Childishness exists in a near absolute state of self-preoccupation. The childish person conceives the world to be run by push buttons placed there for his own convenience. The people with whom he is associated are expected to perform as automatons of his own will. If they do not, he holds them to be faulty. It is not that they are exercising their right to be individuals. As he sees it they are simply out of order. If they cannot be straightened out they will be cast aside as scrap.

Love Is Mindful of Others

Love seeks friends, not courtiers. The person whose

goal it is to love will orient his life to others instead of to self. Fannie Hurst gives us an intimate glimpse into her marriage as she reports an incident which took place between her and her husband. The two of them were having dinner together when he related a decision he had made earlier that day. Struck by her husband's selfless spirit, Fannie burst out, "How is it that in all the years I never remember you doing a thing I wish you hadn't done? How can you be so consistently mindful of others?" Most of us probably do not have so enviable a record, but it is a model toward which to strive. To be consistently mindful of others is a mark of maturity.

We will be surprised to discover that when we alter our childish ways of relating to others, associations presently filled with discord and subject to rupture become harmonious and a source of mutual benefit. Love deserves a chance. Too long we've allowed self to have its childish way. The results have been disappointing, and, in some cases, tragic. Now it is time to try love's "more excellent way."

HELPS FOR STUDY

Goals

To deal with the elements of childishness that are in each of us.

To strengthen qualities of mutual trust, regard, forbearance, appreciation, and concern.

Questions to Discuss

1. In what sense is there some childishness in everyone? How is this good? How is this a problem?

2. When is ambition good? When is it harmful?

70

[handwritten top margin: Christ said greatest is least in his Service]

3. Is it generally better to relate to someone as a companion or as a servant? How so?

4. What does true love do to help overcome the negative qualities of childishness?

5. When a person feels mean, unthankful, impatient, untrusting, uncaring about others—does this mean he is a sinner? Why do you answer as you do?

Learning Activities

1. Get a mirror and look at your reflection in it. What do you see there? What childlike qualities do you find in your life that are good? What qualities in this area would you like to move away from?

2. Jesus taught us to become as little children. Think about some little children you know rather well right now or go and observe some for a while. What qualities in them would you leave to childhood and which would you keep into adult years?

3. Get with some partners and agree upon and write out some prescriptions for dealing with selfish ambition, temperamentalism, tryanny, impatience, thanklessness, intolerance, lack of trust.

[handwritten: set up small (3-4) groups — and spend 5-7" on 3 or 4 of topics]

Love Means You Have To Say, "I'm Sorry"

ONE OF THE MOST popular movies of recent times was a film which had as its theme, "Love Means You Never Have to Say 'I'm Sorry.'" Marked both by profanity and pathos the movie traced the turbulent romance of two college students. Free-spirited and hard as nails the sweetheart of the story resisted her suitor's apologies on grounds that their relationship was not dependent upon such amenities. Hence, she was more inclined to swear at him in subtle humor if he offered an apology than to embrace him in forgiveness.

Make-Believe Love

While the author of this now famous line would defend it on the grounds of realism, one may well ask whether it is realism at all. Dare I suggest that it is a make-believe world in which we may injure others without consequence? "Love Means You Never Have to Say, 'I'm Sorry.'" It's a beautiful thought, at least in the context of a romantic movie. It certainly is a consoling thought in real life when we've committed

72

a transgression. But what is the end result of such total irresponsibility? Fancified love doesn't stand up well under everyday wear and tear on human relationships.

The Bible gives us an entirely different thought on the issue at hand. James writes, "Confess your faults one to another, and pray one for another, that ye may be healed" (5:16). Far from ignoring the wrongs we have done, God tells us we had better get straight to the business of making them right. If we've injured another, our relationships with him and God are in jeopardy and we must take the pains to rectify matters.

Irresponsibility

Why can't we just write off the offense, simply shrug our shoulders and say, "He [she] loves me. He understands. He'll overlook it"? Isn't that really saying, "Since he [she] loves me, I can get away with murder. Here's one relationship I can abuse, be reckless with. Here's an excuse for disregarding common courtesy and kindness."

"After all, love is blind, you know!" What license we find in that! "Love suffereth long and is kind," but it is not numb. "Love . . . seeketh not her own . . . endureth all things," but it has feelings. Who is it that is blind when we hurt others without so much as a word of recompense? Perhaps *we* are the ones who cannot see, who are blind to our crudity, our ruthlessness, our selfishness.

Show me a marriage in which the husband never says, "I'm sorry," and chances are I can show you a wife who bears a thousand scars upon her spirit. Show me a congregation in which the members never say,

"I'm sorry," and I'll show you a fellowship that is shallow and characterized more by hypocritical tolerance than by genuine warmth and affection.

Small offenses piled one upon another kindle a fire that someday a single spark may ignite. A young man who described his father as mean and oppressive told me how that as a teen-ager he had taken all the abuse he could bear. He said, "I made up my mind to get a gun and go home and kill him. It is a wonder I didn't." What we need to do is clear away the kindling as it builds up with day-to-day infractions. And that's part of what James is telling us to do in advocating that we confess our faults.

Apology Heals

To put it another way, saying "I'm sorry" is like pouring precious, soothing ointment on an ugly wound. "Confess your faults that you may be *healed*," says the writer. Nothing is so effective in restoring a relationship to wholeness as a forthright, unqualified apology. And the miracle is that both the offended and the offender are healed. One is healed by the apology and the other by the forgiveness. Thus each serves as the other's physician, each ministers to the other.

There is no more beautiful example of what I've just stated than this personal story told by Denson Franklin. He writes, "I remember a revival in my boyhood. My home church had not grown for years. It was stymied by deep-seated prejudices, hates and conflict. Dr. L. D. Patterson came there for a revival. He decided to stay until victory was won. It was the second week before anything broke. Then he had a service of forgiveness. He invited to the front every man who had known enemies but was willing to forgive them. One of the prominent businessmen came down the aisle in tears. He stood there for a moment. The atmosphere was charged with excitement. Everyone knew his enemy and of the years of conflict. Would he come? Then he came down. Those men—locked in each others arms—cried away their differences. Then others came and embraced before the altar. It was the change in the life of the church and city."[1]

Why should any of us deny himself and others the healing that takes place when we say, "I'm sorry"? Seldom is the love of God so shed abroad in our hearts as it is when we confess our faults.

Learning to Seek Reconciliation

Tragically, many people have never learned to say, "I'm sorry." We find a thousand excuses for ignoring the simple, scriptural formula for having happy homes and churches. We tell ourselves it would never work. It would just be opening ourselves up to scorn and judgment. We probably don't really believe this. If we do, we're dangerously lacking in faith in God's wisdom and man's basic decency. Our real problem is pride. Most of us would rather sleep on thorns than admit we're wrong. But that only points out our immaturity.

Most of us claim spirituality on the wrong grounds, that we never have occasion to say we are sorry. James knows better. His words are for Christians, not the heathens, and the real Christian is the one who can

---

[1]Denson Franklin, *Faith For These Troubled Times* (Westwood, N.J.: Fleming H. Revell, 1953) p. 62.

face up to this "hard saying" and practice it when it strikes home. Hudson tells us, "Those who never seek or offer forgiveness either relate to others on a very superficial basis or never obey God rebuilding broken or disturbed relationships."[2]

During a series of revival meetings, I took a moment one evening to suggest one of my books to the congregation. After the service, sales were rather brisk. The following evening one of the more active members of the church held up his copy of the book and said, "There's a picture of me in here on page 44." It so happened that page 44 marked the beginning of Chapter V, "Becoming a Forgiving Person." This good man then explained to me that for weeks he had been bearing ill will toward his supervisor, whose critical evaluation, he felt, had cost him a salary increase. After reading what I had had to say, he knew exactly what he must do. Before the week was over, he walked into his boss' office and stated his business. His supervisor was most receptive, saying, "I'm glad you came in. This has been bothering me too." A wholesome dialogue followed as each man came to a new appreciation for the other. That evening it was a happy man who told me the conclusion of the matter.

Ailing from Alienation

Painful though it may be to confess our faults, the consequences of refusing to do so are even more costly. Harold Sherman has written a book titled *Your Key to Happiness* in which he cites the relationship between

[2]R. Lofton Hudson, *Helping Each Other Be Human* (Waco, Texas: Word Books, 1970), p. 176.

what a man thinks and how he feels. He uses a personal experience to illustrate this. He was employed to revise an important radio presentation with the promise that he would be given a contract for a permanent job. He invested several months in the assignment. However, when it was finished, he was given no further consideration. In fact, the material which he had produced was used without credit to him. He became exceedingly bitter over this. At length he developed an infection in his throat. Even with the finest medical services he did not recover. Later, he came to pray for those who had wronged him. As he overcame his hatred for them his affliction disappeared. It is written into our nervous systems, "Confess your faults one to another, and pray for one another that ye may be healed."

Hard as it is to ask forgiveness, even this may be easier than extending forgiveness. Love not only means you have to say, "I'm sorry." It also means you have to accept the sorries of others.

Fear of Being Close

There's something very impersonal about this business of never having to say, "I'm sorry." If you never have to apologize to me, I never have to decide what to do with an apology. My feelings can remain unclarified. Moreover, I may even consider myself excused for whatever ill will I may bear toward you. Your apology puts me on the spot. It challenges the love I profess for you. It's far simpler to evade the whole business with a jestful oath (which just may

77

betray more anger than I'm willing to admit). Jenny strikes me as being afraid to be close to anyone and forgiveness brings people together. Why is our society so afraid of a little tenderness?

Even in the church do we not sometimes shy away from emotional involvement with others, almost secretly hoping that the person who has done us wrong will not say he is sorry? How could we forgive him without seeming maudlin? And so what do we do? We send out word on the grapevine that we consider that which he did or said as really nothing, nothing at all. We're not bothered in the least. No sir! And when we see him we put on a happy face—maybe kid a little bit and keep the conversation just as superficial as possible. If he had any thoughts of an apology we've confused him or hindered him in getting on with it.

Be Approachable

One of the most gracious things we can do is to make it easier for persons to apologize to us. This does not mean demanding an apology or hinting that one is in order. It means being authentic about our hurts, honest in our conversation, gentle in our attitude, perceptive in our listening. It's never hard to apologize to someone who already has his arms out to you.

Because we are afraid of the closeness that asking and receiving forgiveness brings we sweep many conflicts under the rug including those within the church. We become great pretenders instead of great lovers. On the surface there appears to be sweet accord, but underneath resentment is building.

78

Work Through Resentment

While I was leading a ministers' conference, a pastor came to me to discuss a great trial he was having. His congregation was split right down the middle over what appeared to be a rather small matter. After pouring out his heart for a few minutes, he exclaimed, "These people never forgive. You think you've gotten everything straightened out, then something happens and it comes out all over again." That's the price we pay for glossing over our animosities. Two contending families reportedly formed the nucleus of this dispute. I rather suspect that although each former controversy supposedly had been resolved, the parties to it were careful to keep their distance. Thus there had never been reconciliation, only the effecting of a momentary truce.

No man can order his heart to forgive. He can only suggest reasons for doing so. And he will need an iron-clad case to convince his emotions they should be anything other than perverse. You may call it forgiveness by trying to overlook it. You may call it forgiveness by brushing the apology aside with a shallow remark such as, "That's okay. We all make mistakes." But if the forgiveness is going to stick, you'll have to get your feelings as well as your intellect involved in the process. Therefore, persons who genuinely wish to be significant to one another can never tolerate a pact between them outlawing discussion of their grievances. Love not only means that I have to say I'm sorry. It also means we'll have to keep on dialoging until my apology is accepted in your innermost parts. Let's not confuse being the church with going to the movies.

HELPS FOR STUDY

Goals

To draw on the resources of forgiveness as a means of Christian growth.

To understand and use more effectively tools for developing responsible relationships such as honesty, openness, forgiveness.

Questions to Discuss

1. What does Jesus really teach when he asks us to forgive seventy times seven?

2. It is common today to speak of those people who are "alienated" from others, from Christ, from their world. What does the term mean in these cases?

3. What all would you include in understanding the meaning of "reconciliation"? How does salvation fit in here?

4. In what sense does apology heal the one who apologizes as well as the one who receives the apology?

5. Have you noticed a fear of being close in people? What causes this?

Learning Activities

1. Work out in some form—by writing, talking through, or acting out—some skits on one person asking forgiveness of another. Demonstrate some of the problems involved for both the asker and the receiver.

2. Think of some of the most approachable people you know. What makes them this way? appearance? expression on their faces? what they say? attitude of friendliness and concern? How approachable was Jesus? Offer evidence. How can Christians become more approachable?

The Shape Of Love

MANY OF US would agree that Jesus was the master relater. That doesn't mean that everyone loved him, or that he was a great PR (public relations) man, but it does mean that he related to people with such intensity that he provoked from all of them the true nature of their relationship with him. It is doubtful if there was ever a phony relationship with Jesus Christ. I don't think many of us could say that. The rich ruler was perhaps superficial in his approach to Christ. Jesus swept aside the "good Master bit" and tested this young man's sincerity by asking him to give his wealth to the poor.

Relationships in Process

Now because Jesus was and is the master relater, we might expect to find from among his associations, a model relationship. And I would like to suggest his relationship with Peter as such a model. Certainly with the possible exception of John the Beloved, Jesus was closer to Peter than to any other mortal being. I realize the model I suggest is open to question because of the spotty performance of Peter. By way of justification, I would say that it serves as a worthy model, not because of what it tells us about Peter; but because

81

of what it tells us about Jesus. Not because it was a perfect relationship, but, to the contrary, because it affords us an invaluable lesson in how to sustain a relationship under less than ideal conditions. It was a stormy relationship what with Peter's protest against Jesus washing his feet and his argument against Christ's fatal return to Jerusalem. It was an on-again, off-again relationship what with Peter's denial. However, ultimately and finally it was a prevailing relationship. I suspect that if those relationships which you and I hope to have with our spouses, with our children, with our friends, and with those of the church are to be as creative as we would like them to be, it just might be that they will not be as patently perfect as we have presumed they should be. Instead, they will be dynamic and always in process.

Andras Angyal very helpfully gives us three characteristics of a loving relationship. (1) The experience of a certain fundamental belongingness and unity between the lover and the loved. (2) A recognition and acceptance of the otherness or difference of the person loved. (3) An understanding of a very special kind of the nature of the person loved.* Now let us apply those three characteristics to the relationship which existed between Jesus and Peter.

Belonging to One Another

First, the experience of a certain fundamental belongingness and unity between the lover and the loved. The aim of love is togetherness, and it is prepared to

---

*Andras Angyal, *Neurosis and Treatment* (New York: John Wiley & Sons, 1965) p. 25.

pay a King's ransom to provide for and to preserve that togetherness. The belongingness and unity which Jesus experienced with his disciples shines through his words again and again. As he prepared to take his leave from the disciples, Christ commended them to the keeping of the Holy Spirit. As he prays to the Father he says, "Those which thou hast given me I have kept and none of them is lost, save the son of perdition." In a sobering moment with Peter, Jesus said, "I have prayed for thee, Peter, that thy faith fail not." Jesus' relationship with the disciples personified the relationship God had sought to have with Israel and beautifully illustrates the jealousy he confessed for them.

To love another person is to identify with him. It is to have a stake in his life as you have a stake in your own life. It is to think corporately. It is to have a "we" feeling about the two of you. It is to share your life with another and to hope his life will be shared with you. It is a matter of inclusion rather than exclusion.

Integrity Preserved

Now, identification does not automatically mean mutuality. It is not necessarily a case of monkey see, monkey do. For example, Jesus loved the world. There was an identification there, a "we" feeling that made him quite comfortable as he sat down to eat with the Publicans and the sinners. And yet, we know that Jesus was never a party to their perversion.

One of the dearest, most godly women that I have ever known has a wayward brother who has tasted

83

the dregs of degradation. No two lives could ever be any more diverse in their pattern than those two. Yet this woman has a unity and a belongingness with her brother which makes his mishaps real to her. She has little mutuality, but much identification.

We need to participate in the *effect* experiences of others, even if not the *cause* experiences. By that I mean; we may not have been a participant in another's indiscretion but we can be a participant in the agony of his subsequent dilemma. Although we are not responsible, we will hurt with him and if he is the victim of circumstances not of his own making, and circumstances not common to us, we will likewise feel his reproach and share his struggle.

Loving the Unconventional

The church's love has perhaps been most weak at those points where there should have been identification but not mutuality. We have done a superlative job of loving those whose spiritual and moral values were in sympathy with ours. This is the glory of the church. But the shame of the church is that we have sometimes held in contempt those whose values were contrary to ours. As a matter of fact, we have on occasion assumed it was our responsibility to *condemn these people,* instead of in *redeeming them.* It is never enough for us to weep over those who weep and to rejoice over those who rejoice so long as they are our own kind. We must do the same for those who have nothing to commend them to our corporation, for they too are God's offspring, even if errant children. A disciplined love gives us perspective on people in their

84

faults and strengths, to understand, accept, and deal realistically with them. We say a great deal about ourselves when we declare whether the prodigal son ought to be barred from our door or embraced in our arms.

Respect for Difference

Secondly, let us consider Angyal's reference to the recognition and acceptance of the difference or otherness of the person loved. As surely as God made us, he made us individually. There was only one Adam. There is only one you and only one me. It seems that it was God's intent to fashion each of us as a unique self unlike any other. Despite his commanding charisma, Jesus never infringed upon the rights of his disciples. He never usurped their God-given sovereignty. He said to Peter, "Satan hath desired to have thee." But he didn't say, "I am not going to let him have you." Peter was allowed to follow Jesus afar off. He was free to position himself near the enemy campfire, free to curse and say, "I never knew him." Even though the consequences were dire, Jesus would not be a dictator.

To love a man is to let him be himself. No matter how great our stake in his life, we will resist the almost irresistible urge to make him but an automation of our own will. No matter how great our togetherness with another, we must respect that line where the "we" ends and the "I" begins in his life. Identification does not mean possession. It is not a contradiction to say that two persons can share their lives without either of them sacrificing his personality.

One time a rather strong-willed young lady introduced her fiance to me. I had the strangest feeling as we stood there talking that she had her hand in the back of his coat and was pulling the strings. It was as if the words I heard him saying were really coming from her and that he even batted his eyes as directed by her. Love? Well, maybe on an immature level; but not the kind of love that leads to satisfaction and fulfillment.

Room for Individuality

If we love another person we will work for his good within the framework of his choice; just as God works for our good within the framework of our given life-situation. Let us have none of this Now-I'm-ready-to-help-you-anytime-you-see-it-my-way kind of manipulation. Concern is no longer godly jealousy when it asks homage as the price of concern. "All of these things I will give unto you if you will bow down and worship me." Sounds like some of the love we give, doesn't it? I need not remind you those were not the words of Jesus. They belong to Satan.

Do you give love as a strong limb on which to sit or as a cage in which to imprison? If we love as Jesus loved we'll loose those we love to let them soar and dive. Only in this way can they develop. This is not being indifferent, no more than it was indifference on the part of Barnabas to let John Mark throw in the sponge and go home. It is the most dedicated, God-like form of love known to man. Of course this requires that we remain ready to reinstate, restore, and

86

guide according to the need and desire of the other person.

Love Heightens Perception

Thirdly, there is the matter of understanding; understanding of a very special kind. I think you have probably already observed that when one person loves another, there comes to him an intuition about that other person's feelings, needs, and capabilities. Jesus understood Peter better than that rugged fisherman understood himself. Here is Peter declaring his undying fidelity, "I am ready to go with you to prison and to the death," to which Jesus sadly shakes his head and answers, "Oh, no, Peter, you over-estimate yourself. Before this day ends, you will deny me three times." Yet over against this, Jesus adds, "when thou art converted, strengthen the brethren." Jesus, you see, understood not only Peter's perfidy, but also his promise. He saw beyond his unfaithfulness.

When we really love someone, we see his faults but we also see his virtues—even those that have not yet surfaced. We see in him what no one else sees. We are told that love is blind. It is not that love is blind; it is just that love appears to be blind because it "thinketh no evil." In fact, love has an extraordinary insight and can see diamonds where other people see only soot. To identify with others is to covet their development. The minute you take someone unto you, you want the best for them and you want to help them emerge as the great person God intended them to be.

When Helen Keller was nineteen months old, she suffered a dastardly illness which as you well know

87

left her without hearing and sight. Inevitably in a short time she lost her ability to speak. When she was six years old her parents took her to Dr. Alexander Graham Bell to consult with him as to what kind of an education might be given her. Dr. Bell suggested that they take her to a young lady whose name was Ann Sullivan. Ann herself had been blind but had partially recovered her sight. On March 2, 1887, Miss Sullivan officially became Helen Keller's private teacher, establishing a relationship which was to exist until 1936 when Ann died—49 years later. During that time Helen Keller's abilities came to the fore. She blossomed into a brilliant intellect and authoress whose adventuresome life and whose stupendous achievements dwarf yours and mine. Ann Sullivan must have loved Helen Keller a great deal, don't you think, to have seen in this pathetic little, blind, deaf, speechless child such great potential and to painstakingly help bring it out.

Love Looks for the Best

We must love others not only for what they are but for what they can be. Real love is incurably optimistic and hopelessly futuristic. Crosses are always carried in advance, you know, on the supposition that there is a value there worth saving. Love and redemption are inseparable. Only love yields the faith that yields the sacrifice that yields the transformation. On the other hand, love and judgmentalism can't be put together. Love looks for good while judgment looks for evil.

One time when he was criticized for befriending a

young man with a rather disreputable reputation the president of the Armour Packing Company said, "Well, we haven't struck pay dirt yet, but I think there is a streak of gold in him somewhere." Two people looked at the same man but they saw quite different things. One looked with an eye to love and the other with an eye to judge. May we pray for the eye to love?

explain why

HELPS FOR STUDY

Goals

To gain an understanding of how love contributes to unity among people, acceptance of each other, and understanding of each other.

To grow in understanding of how love strengthens the ties between God and us.

Questions to Discuss

1. What keeps you from or helps you love all the more someone who is quite different from you?

2. How strongly are we called to love that which is unconventional? that which is quite different from us? that which seeks to express its own individuality strongly?

3. What would you say was the most model human relationship Jesus had? The author suggests Peter despite of or because of the up-and-down quality of Peter's relationship to Jesus.

4. How much place in the Christian scheme of things is there for the person who rebels against the normal patterns of behavior? for the person who is a nonconformist?

Learning Activities

1. Test out key concepts of unity, acceptance, and understanding in the love that exists between different kinds of persons. Think of your own loving relationships. Think of people mentioned in this chapter such as Ann Sullivan and Helen Keller. Test out people you know.

89

2. Test out the basis for any love relationship with the following:

a. Young, dirty, strange clothes, extremely long and unkempt hair, anger showing in the eyes.

b. Someone just about like you in age, appearance, interests, opinions.

c. An old man who doesn't speak your language, follows another religion.

Listening
With Love

INDIANA not long ago inaugurated a governor who had campaigned on the slogan, "He hears you." About the same time as the election campaign, one of the Big Three automobile manufacturers ran a nation-wide public relations promotion proclaiming the slogan, "We listen better."

I suspect market researchers have discovered that the American public does not feel it is being listened to very well. Isn't it interesting that the way to win an election and the way to sell an automobile is to tell the people that you are a good listener. That really is not a terribly imposing requisite since it is within reach of everyone. Evidently, being listened to means a great deal to us. We are tired of being manipulated by big business and big government, of being the pawns of those who are insensitive to our feelings and unsympathetic to our needs. We want to be heard. Therefore we give patronage to those who pledge to listen.

Want to be Heard

What is true of us collectively, is true of us individually. You and I don't want to be heard just by the great impersonal forces of society. We want to be heard singularly by those particular persons important to our respective lives; by our friends, our family, our

91

employers or employees, our teachers, our neighbors, our pastors, and others whose support we need.

You are familiar with the story of Esther. She being a queen and wife of the Persian king was called upon to intercede in behalf of her people, the Jews. In the King's response to Esther's appeal we find that this man, who might have been considered a pagan, nonetheless has something to teach us about being a good listener.

Even as we want to be heard by others, we must ourselves be good listeners. This being true, we will need some comprehension of what it takes to make a good listener. From the listener's standpoint, what conditions are conducive to good communication?

Attentive Listening

Good listening involves being attentive. When you listen to someone, listen as though at that moment he were the most important person to you in all the world. Now, you are not required to listen to him endlessly, but during that span of time which you give him, give him all of it. A begrudging listener is not a good listener.

As Esther approached the king, he greeted her thus: "What is it? What is your request, Queen Esther? It shall be yours even to half of my kingdom" (Esther 5:6). This man was accustomed to receiving chiefs of state. Still he welcomed his wife as cordially as he might have any potentate no matter how powerful the nation represented. For the period of Esther's audience with the king, the affairs of government ground to a halt and she had his undivided attention.

It seems to me that some of us who are careful to speak with courtesy ofttimes listen with rather poor manners. We listen inattentively. To do so is an insult to the person addressing us. We thus imply that his presence is tolerated rather than welcomed. We make of his thoughts, foolishness, and his words, babble.

A young father was sharing recently how that his six-year-old daughter is quite perceptive as to how carefully others listen to her. This fact is a very strategic one regarding the young lady's musical education. Her parents have discovered that she does not do well for a teacher who fails to listen with interest when she talks. However, she does superbly for the teacher who proves to be a good listener as well as instructor. We have a clue here as to why each of us performs as he does. Those who listen to us with respect bring out the best in us. Others do not.

Hearing Is Accepting

Freedom of speech does not mean a great deal without free acceptance. What does it matter that I have a right to speak my opinion if nobody is interested in hearing it? My words are symbols of me and if my words are minimized I feel personally diminished. If you want to flatter someone, listen to him. In the simple act of listening you are saying to him, "You are important to me." Listening is a ministry of recognition and all of us need to both give and receive of this ministry.

Ted Williams, the baseball great, recalls his first introduction to Jim Thorpe, the legendary Indian athlete. Thorpe was sixty-five; Williams was still a young man. He says, "Right off I was carried away with Thorpe . . . I was so impressed with how quiet and attentive he was, how he would listen to people. Here's Jim Thorpe, all-time, all-time, and he'd listen to anybody. He'd smile and he'd laugh and he'd listen."*

Not always must we say something to serve. Our churches are full of sounds. Everyone seems to be talking, many of us in an effort to be helpful. However, sometimes the most helpful thing we can do is to listen attentively.

Bishop Gerald Kennedy remembers those frustrating, devastating days of his early ministry. His first pastorate sometimes drove him to the very brink of despair. When the burden became heavier than seemingly he could bear, he would walk down the street and tell his troubles to the Congregational-Christian pastor. Bishop Kennedy says that it saved his life.

On the Same Level

Listening is best done as an equal. We do not like others to talk down to us. We resist having to talk up to them.

Esther stood in the inner court of the King. It was the law of the land that anyone coming before the king without invitation was liable to the death penalty. Therefore, in interceding for her people Esther was risking her very life. We can imagine her apprehension. However, the king extended his scepter which of course was a gesture of peace; a way of saying you may come closer; you may speak. How reassuring this must

---

*Ted Williams, *My Turn At Bat* (New York: Pocket Books, 1969), pp. 8-9.

have been to Esther. In that culture as a woman and a member of a subservient race, she was inferior to the king on two counts. Still, he treated her with equality and encouraged her boldness.

In our demeanor it makes a great deal of difference how we receive others. You and I never meet a single person without extending to him either a scepter or a sword. By those little, subtle traits of personality, we invite others either to come or to leave, to speak or to remain silent, to remain erect or to bow. Consequently, some find themselves surrounded by people, others are largely left alone. Simply stated, the haughty and the severe repel, the humble and the meek attract. Those who want counsel and those who want comfort sense where they may receive it and where they may not.

Gentle Listening

I have a good friend who is a top industry executive. He is a splendid person of impeccable character. He has great Christian concern and is exceedingly generous. Yet, there is a bluntness about him, a pile driving directness that some people find intimidating. He is aware of this and he laments it. He even acknowledges that if his employees have a complaint or a problem they don't come to him. They go to his sales manager whose personality is not so threatening as his own. The lesson is that we seek out only those who we conclude love us or who might come to love us.

The doctrine of the priesthood of believers can only be a reality in a church of gentle listeners. We are only going to confess our faults to one another and pray for one another so long as those to whom we would confess measure to standard. The standard is that they not betray us, that they not condemn us, and that they not shame us if we reveal ourselves to them.

Many a spoken word is but a dove in search of dry land. It is a probe. It is an action testing for reaction. If it finds judgmentalism it returns without assurance of refuge. However, if it finds receptiveness and understanding, it returns with joy, bearing an olive sprig.

Why is it, do you suppose, that the publicans and sinners could comfortably sit at meat with Jesus and even own their sins in his presence, while they could not do this in the presence of the Pharisees? The answer is, of course, that Jesus listened without ever arching an eyebrow, without ever clicking his tongue or raising his voice. If you would be one to whom others speak freely, then Jesus must become your example.

Trust Is a Must

We deal our words to those who will not play them against us. It is an honor to serve in the role of listener. You may be sought out in the night as Jesus was by Nicodemus, or you may be conscripted solely on the basis of your proximity. You may be chosen after a long period of observation or you may be elected spontaneously because of great urgency. No matter how it happens yours is a sacred trust. Keep it with all diligence.

For several years I had recurring opportunities to minister to a wandering alcoholic who had served time in the penitentiary. He had never really come to peace with God or with himself. One time he said to his loving sister, "Pastor Huttenlocker is the only man in all my life that I have been able to talk to." Who knows what his life might have been had someone been a kindly listener to him many years ago.

Listening and Feeling

Listening is also to be done with great sensitivity. We ought not to listen dispassionately or impersonally as though totally detached from the speaker. We ought to listen with empathy. We should be able to identify with the speaker. When Esther finished speaking to the king it was as though he were himself a Jew. He so related to the plight of the Jews as Esther described it that he at once issued an order canceling Haman's plans to annihilate all Hebrews residing in Persia.

You really haven't listened to anyone until you have heard the cry of his heart. That may mean reading between the lines, perhaps decoding his message so that you understand what is disturbing him and destroying him. He may state clearly to you what this is, or he may veil it in the form of a threat or a brag or just simple idle conversation. Whatever the case may be your job is to hear the real message.

I remember a rather benign, elderly citizen of the church who came to me one day, ostensibly to apologize for a very harmless remark that in no way wronged anyone. When he finished apologizing, I encouraged him to linger a bit. Soon he said, "Pastor, sometimes I feel as though I don't do anything right." Raised by an extremely authoritarian father, married to a wife who treated him as a child, he felt as though he couldn't even speak without asking permission and here he had spoken out of turn. I took advantage of that opportunity to affirm his worth as a person. I emphasized that he had some rights and privileges which were sacredly his as a human individual. He left my office feeling ten feet tall. No, he was not instantaneously cured of his feelings of inadequacy, far from it. However, had I simply accepted his apology I would have reinforced rather than weakened those feelings.

Communication Keeps Us Company

Listening lessens the isolation that is felt by the speaker. All the deep emotions of life have to be shared: love, joy, sorrow, fear, anger, anticipation, and the rest. They have to be shared to be assimilated. Therefore, we communicate in order to experience community. What you and I *feel* while listening determines the depth of our response. We may listen and say, "Oh my," or if more appropriate, "How wonderful." But if deep down inside we don't feel "Oh my" or "How wonderful," the speaker knows he has not really been heard and his isolation remains with him. Maybe that is what the scripture means when it says to weep with those who weep and rejoice with those who rejoice (Rom. 12:15).

In the incident of Lazarus' death we have a revealing study in human relations. Mary and Martha brought their grief to Jesus. We see that before the Master said anything, before he did anything, he *felt* something. He wept. That describes our High Priest as one who is instantaneously touched with the feelings of our infirmities (Heb. 4:15). Let us listen as Jesus did.

Hawthorne once said, "I have reached the seldom trod places of their hearts and found the well spring of their tears." It takes a lot of listening to be able to say that.

HELPS FOR STUDY

Goals

To gain skill in listening with love.

To understand the importance of communication in expressing love and ministering to people.

Questions to Discuss

1. What does it really mean to listen?
2. Can you really hear people without accepting them, being on a basis of trust? How so or not so?
3. What does "gentle listening" mean to you?
4. How is it possible to accept people, to show trust in them, and to identify with them clearly without seeming to approve wrongdoing, shortcomings, and various problems in their lives?

Learning Activities

1. If you can be with even a small group play the game "Gossip" to demonstrate some of the problems that go with listening. Get in a circle and various people start brief messages of varying degree of complexity by whispering them—not always too loudly or clearly—in their neighbor's ear. The neighbor passes along what he thought he heard to the next person and so on. After the message has circulated, discuss together how it changed and why.

2. Practice listening to someone tell about a concern or problem he has. Keep track of what both of you do to communicate. Consider the barriers to real listening. Consider how personal understandings are bound up in listening.

Dialogues In Love

Part I

LISTEN TO ALL the conversations of the world, those between nations as well as those between couples," challenges Paul Tournier, "They are for the most part dialogues of the deaf." Dialogues of the deaf—what a graphic way of saying that everyone is talking but no one is listening. If no one is listening perhaps we need to change our manner of speaking. We are like a broadcasting station which sends out programs that are of little interest to listeners or perhaps even offensive to them. Such a station gets tuned out. How then can we get our broadcasts heard?

Knowing and Being Known

There are certain requisites which, if learned and applied, will earn us the listening we seek. A good conversation is one in which those parties involved become open to one another. That is, each may reveal his true self to the other—his values, his feelings, his convictions—to whatever degree is appropriate to that conversation.

What conditions encourage that kind of openness? Experience tells us there are two. The first is that the conversation be self-validating. The second is that it be nonthreatening. In this chapter we shall discuss only the former. We will deal with the latter in the chapter immediately to follow.

What makes a conversation self-validating to you or to me? Very simply, it needs to be one in which we have a stake or hopefully may gain a stake and/or in which we expect to show well.

Will This Interest Me?

The above being true, a good conversation is one in which the topic is of interest to us. Apart from some avid interest in another party to the conversation (i.e., a romantic inclination or perhaps hero worship) you and I don't become very much involved in conversations the subject of which is on the edge of our lives.

One day Jesus asked his disciples, "Who do men say that I am?" (Matt. 16:13). Do you think they were interested in that topic? Indeed they were, extremely so. One does not forsake his vocation and family to follow another man from city to city for three years without having some rather strong ideas regarding who he is and what he is about. And furthermore, Jesus was the center of attention and the subject of talk wherever he went. The disciples had no doubt waited long for him to raise this question. They wanted to come to grips with it. They wanted to confirm their thoughts.

Now You Are Talking About Me

You and I are just self-centered enough to need some ego involvement in anything we do, even in making conversation. It is very normal for each of us to invest a little bit of himself in those things which give his life meaning—his family, his vocation, perhaps a hobby, and an organization or two. Whenever conversation turns to one of these things in which any of us has invested himself, it is as though he were himself being talked about. Consequently, he becomes deeply involved in the discussion (although at this point he may or may not be completely open).

Not very long ago I was having dinner with a group of ministers. The baseball World Series was being played. One of the men around the table came from a city represented in the series by one of the teams. He dominated the conversation that noon as he exuded enthusiasm about his team, talked about the players and past games. It was obvious where he had invested a part of himself. The rest of us listened passively. In due time one of the other pastors, in a most charitable way, showed his growing resistance to the line of conversation as he said something like this, "Who wins the World Series doesn't matter to me. These are only games and I don't consider them very important." Yet, I dare say if the conversation had shifted to the subject of how to have a growing congregation, the second minister would have enjoyed the conversation and contributed much, since this was of primary concern to him and in the area of his competence.

My Topic or Yours?

The things you and I talk about may reveal a fundamental disregard for our listeners. We don't talk about the things that interest them. We talk about the things that interest us. It is essential to becoming a good communicator that a person move beyond the narrow confines of his own life into the concerns and interests of the lives of others.

When, for example, we engage in conversation which consists basically of self-pity or bragging we lose our audience. The reason for this is, of course, because the conversation centers so exclusively and so overwhelmingly on us. Others may listen for a brief time to our laments or boasts providing we later allow them their turn.

An actor rose from obscurity to great fame. One day he ran into an old friend whom he had not seen for years. This illustrious, popular figure engaged in an extensive monologue explaining to his friend just how it was that he had come to wealth and prominence. Being a bit embarrassed about his self-infatuation, he said to his friend, "Oh, but here we are talking about me. Let's talk about you. How did you like my latest movie?" If we are not really interested in others it is difficult to be a good communicator even though we try.

Between Brothers

Next, let us consider the relational aspect of dialogue. A good conversation is one in which each participant is made to feel equal. A bank president and a custodian may meet in the corridor at the close of day, but if there is to be meaningful communication between them in that moment and in that setting, position must be laid aside and their meeting be as man to man.

Jesus said to his disciples, "Who do you think that I am?" (Matt. 16:15). He was flattering their intuition. He was saying to them, "What you think of me is important." Jesus had the mind of God. Peter had the mind of a fisherman. Yet Jesus was willing to place his mind on the level of the fisherman's in order to relate to Peter.

We are validated as persons by those situations which allow for our input. If we have nothing to contribute we may well ask if we are needed. If we are not needed we may well ask if we are significant. It is unescapable that the price tag I place upon myself, that is, what I consider myself to be worth, is in part influenced by what I have to offer the world. I must feel that I have something to contribute in order to feel significant.

What Do You Think?

Recall the earlier reference to the listening campaign of the Indiana governor. During the days prior to election, numerous paid telecasts featured the candidate being quizzed by concerned citizens of Indiana. In each of the broadcasts he gave his view but then always closed by asking the interviewer, "What do you think?" It was wise strategy and it will work for any of us. If you want others to listen to you also invite their comment.

Church school teachers and others, too, should be aware that it is best not to say all there is to be said about any given thing, because when you do, the other person is left with no opportunity to contribute. The speaker becomes the "know it all" and the listener becomes the "know nothing." It is also a good idea to avoid the categorical statement or tone. When you speak with a "that's that" kind of finality you preclude any further conversation. You imply that anything else is either redundant or in error. We are indebted to Eric Berne for helping us see the effect of relationship upon communication. According to Dr. Berne, each time we speak to another it is either as parent-to-child, or adult-to-adult, or child-to-adult. To speak to another adult as parent-to-child is degrading to him and will not produce constructive communication. Strive, rather, to speak as on a par with your listener.

Love Me, Love My Words

A physician in our congregation illustrates the principle of listening as an equal by recalling one of his professors in medical school, a brilliant fellow who was acknowledged by his peers as one of the greatest among them. It seems that whenever anyone was aghast at this man's understanding or his knowledge of medicine he would respond by saying, "Oh, one of my interns taught me that." How well do you suppose that professor's students listened to him? No doubt they listened carefully because he dignified them by the implication that they had contributed to his competence even as he was contributing to theirs.

Daring to Be Human

Finally, a good conversation is one in which the parties thereto display genuine humility. If I am to reveal my true self to you, fortunately or unfortunately, it will soon become apparent to you just how human I am. I cannot be very comfortable about that unless you respond by showing some of your humanity, thus preserving the equality of our relationship. Within the family of God there should be a great deal of dependency upon one another for prayer and counsel. This is best encouraged by mutual sharing.

Jesus often shared his humanity with his disciples. They had ample opportunity to see the fleshly side of the Son of God. For example, he said to the woman at the well, "Give me to drink." He showed impatience with the disciples for their slowness to learn and for their occasional faithlessness. As they went together into the Garden of Gethsemane to pray, Jesus laid bare his anguish as he said, "My soul is exceedingly sorrowful, even unto death."

A Happy Face May Hide a Hypocrite

Contrary to the way most of us function (even in church), Jesus did not imply or teach that we must always put on a happy face. Instead he let others know the pathos he was experiencing at any given moment. This is important, because you and I can best accept our humanity when in the presence of others who accept theirs. It is very easy for me to hate myself with all of my negative feelings when I am around people who seem immune to weakness. But around those who are earthly, those who are not threatened by their humanity but who believe in themselves despite their limitations, I begin to accept my limitations and to find some degree of courage that I may yet be the person I aspire to be.

The preacher who takes a hard line against the sinner, who places himself above doubt, anxiety, lust, or anger will be very popular with those in his audience

106

who are striving hard to avoid any confrontation with the unresolved conflicts in their own lives. And in telling them that they have to be perfect all at once he saves them from any consideration as to whether or not they are. (It would be unbearable to entertain the notion they are not.) That same preacher, however, will not be well received by those who are striving diligently, objectively, and honestly to cope with the unresolved conflicts in their lives. He will have nothing helpful to say to them by glossing over reality. More than that, they are going to suspect him of being phony.

Risking Rejection

To be a good communicator we have to take risks. To reveal yourself to others is to expose yourself to rejection, since they may not like that true self you show them. Only the secure can tolerate risk. Therefore, fundamental to becoming a good communicator is the development of a strong sense of self worth, so that you dare to be honest about yourself.

Honesty in communication is vital because we relate most deeply to one another, not at the level of intellect, but at the level of feeling. For example, two people can talk about the weather but it will not bring them together even if they both agree that it is a lovely day. Conversely, if they talk about their respective struggles they will find a blessed bond developing between them even though their struggles may be quite different. Only as we are known can we be loved.

Finding Acceptance

Bruce Larson, in his little book *Alive Now,* relates

107

an incident that came out of a prayer and Bible study group which a concerned young Christian housewife had organized in a suburban neighborhood. It was the objective of this person to win her neighbors to Jesus Christ. It seemed as though she was not making any progress whatsoever. She was inclined to feel the other women were hopeless. Then one morning she and her husband had what was for them a rare fight. The group was to meet that afternoon. Her first impulse was not to go. However, she felt compelled. No sooner had the meeting begun than did she blurt out her confessional about what had happened that morning. Then she said, "I don't deserve to teach you. I am not even worthy to be here in this condition." Overcome with guilt and emotion she left the meeting feeling as she went that she had lost all influence with the group. To her utter amazement she learned later that three of the women in attendance that morning had made profound Christian growth as a result of her remarks. For the first time they saw her as one of them and concluded that what God meant to her he could mean to them.*

We are so afraid of being human, of being open with one another. And I suppose for good reason. But over against this is our strong yearning to be one with others. What we want so desperately can only happen as we are willing to meet each other as real persons, not as pretences.

———

*Bruce Larson, *Dare to Live Now* (Grand Rapids: Zondervan Publishing House, 1965) p. 46-47.

HELPS FOR STUDY

Goals

To grow in the ability to engage others in conversations that are important and meaningful to them in light of the gospel.

To list elements of Christianity that make daily conversation more meaningful.

Questions to Discuss

1. What does the author mean by "self-validating conversation"?

2. What Christian motivations are involved in becoming a skillful conversationalist on significant subjects?

3. What does it mean to converse as "between brothers"?

4. What are the risks involved in carrying out self-validating conversations?

5. What does this heading mean: "A Happy Face May Hide a Hypocrite"?

Learning Activities

1. Carry out a conversation with a friend and stop and analyze what happened. At what level of depth did you get? What helped the conversation go well? Which one of you tended to lead the conversation? Whose topic was dealt with?

2. Read some conversations in fiction—magazine short stories or books—and analyze them for their importance. Compare them with conversations reported in the Bible.

Dialogues In Love

Part II

COMMUNICATION is like the rain. If there is not enough of it our spirits feel a drought of fellowship. They become barren and desolate. If there is too much we feel inundated by a flood of words and submerged by unassimilated thoughts. If it comes too forcibly great cleavages are eroded in the relationship between speaker and listener. And so good communication is like a gentle shower; falling softly for a season, refreshing, and then subsiding until the soil is again in readiness.

Jesus knew the manner of speaking as a gentle shower. In John 8:3-11 we read about a woman caught in the very act of adultery. The Pharisees brought her to Jesus. They were prepared to stone her for her crime as allowed by the law of Moses. They had already pelted her with accusations. Unobtrusively Jesus intervened. Tenderly he addressed himself to her. To this setting came a sweet peace where only a moment before had been a violent storm.

Denunciation or Dialogue?

What was the secret? Jesus replaced denunciation with dialogue. If you and I would be engaged in more conversations like the one which took place between Jesus and the woman and fewer such as took place between the Pharisees and the woman, we could be following Christ's example. We would be practicing that manner of speaking which is nonthreatening.

So then, what is nonthreatening communication? It might be defined as that form of communication which neither by topic nor tone causes alarm within any participant regarding loss of his autonomy, serenity, or sense of personal worth.

This being true, then, a nonthreatening conversation is devoid of judgment. Judgmentalism immediately creates a hostile atmosphere which precludes any further openness. The Bible repeatedly warns against judging. Jesus said, "Judge not, that ye be not judged" (Matt. 7:1).

How much dialogue do you think took place between the Pharisees and their prisoner? Interestingly enough, not a single word of response is recorded in the Scripture from her. Perhaps there was none. Judgmentalism can create but one of three reactions. (1) Silence, either in the interest of precluding further implication or as a passive act of belligerence. In either case when one of two parties to a conversation becomes silent, obviously there is not going to be much further communication. (2) Defensiveness, which invariably is an emotional, rather than an intellectual, response and, therefore, not usually very objective. (3) Confession, which is pretty unlikely in the presence of judgmentalism, since judgmentalism by its very nature implies a will to prosecute given a shred of evidence.

A woman told of how she went to see her pastor because she was prone to worry. She said that the next

Too many times we're our own worst critic.

Sunday his sermon was a barrage against people who worry, saying they ought to be down on their knees praying before God instead of running around sniveling to everyone. She said, "I was embarrassed to tears. I knew he was talking about me and I thought everyone else there did too."

Atmosphere of Trust

When we are harsh with those who have made their faults known to us, or critical of those who displease us, we take the pose of an enemy. Judgmentalism is threatening because it is usually interpreted as rejection. It identifies for the guilty where the stones will come from.

"My mother does not converse—she lectures," said a seventeen-year-old boy. "She can turn the simplest idea into a complex inquiry. I avoid her," he said. "I don't have time for her long speeches."*

If we want communication, we need to create an atmosphere of trust, which is to say, we come across as persons who would rather help than hurt those who have been found wanting. We must be persons who can accept others even though guilty. Jesus said to this woman, "Neither do I condemn thee." Only when we have said that will we have further opportunity to say, "Go and sin no more." Only when we have gained another person's confidence have we earned the right to counsel him.

*Haim G. Ginott, *Between Parent and Teenager* (Toronto: The MacMillan Company, 1969) p. 42.

112

Controlled Conversation

Secondly, a nonthreatening conversation is one in which emotions are kept under control. A person who has lost his poise is a menacing figure. Anger that rages unbecomingly repels us. In an earlier chapter we noted that the expression of feeling is essential to effective communication. However, too much expression can be damaging to communication. While it is true that we should voice our negative feelings, how we do it is the most treacherous factor in any dialogue. Negative feelings must be subdued before they are verbalized.

During a premarital counseling session, the bride-to-be was upbraiding her fiance for not having more often taken her into his confidence. She had had some therapy and was thoroughly schooled in the value of people being open with one another. "But when I tell you I had a few drinks last night," he protested, "you fly all to pieces." She had appropriately learned that he should confide in her but she had not learned her own obligation when he did so. If she had responded with composure, "That makes me very angry," or "That creates a great deal of anxiety within me," they might have worked on his problem together. As things stood he shielded the truth from her to avoid inciting her.

When we fail to control our emotions we demonstrate that we cannot handle certain realities. We prove ourselves to be poor stewards of openness and are, therefore, not privileged to it.

A young father was pushing a baby carriage down

113

the street. Inside, an infant was screaming loudly. The father kept repeating, "Control yourself, John. Easy does it. Please try to be calm, John." A matronly appearing passerby stopped to compliment this young father, saying, "My, you certainly know how to speak to a baby. So your son's name is John." "Oh, no ma'am," said the father. "His name is Charles. *My* name is John." If we want openness, we do well to acknowledge biblical wisdom which says, "A soft answer turneth away wrath" (Prov. 15:1).

What We Say Includes How We Say It

People respond as much to the feeling tone as to the verbal content of what we say. That means we should not load our voices with more anger or more anxiety than we actually feel. Otherwise, we will appear distraught even though our words do not say so.

I have used this illustration: If the fat blazes up in the frying pan and you scream, "There's a fire!" don't be surprised if someone calls the fire department. When the truck arrives you will probably be embarrassed and say, "I don't understand it. All I said was the fat was burning in the frying pan." Actually you said much more than that. You inferred a dire emergency and that was the response you got. Simply by controlling our voices we can avoid provoking responses we do not feel justified by what we sometimes say.

Free of Manipulation

Thirdly, a nonthreatening conversation is one free of manipulation. The prey in a manipulative conversation may be open to the point at which he becomes suspicious. Thereafter, he will guard what he says and what he reveals.

The Pharisees tried to manipulate Jesus in this conversation. They sought to trap him in a conflict between what the law of Moses said and what Jesus himself advocated. "This they said, tempting him, that they might have to accuse him." Jesus did not give a direct answer. Instead, he knelt down and wrote in the sand.

Manipulation is, of course, an attempt to extract something from another without his awareness or presumably his will. In other words, the conversation has a hidden agenda which is known to the speaker but not to the listener.

A father and a son were engaged in a conversation initiated by the father to manipulate the son. The son became aware of this, hence, countering with a statement of fact each irrational statement by the father. Soon the father became frustrated, then irritated. He said, "This isn't getting us anywhere. We are just going around in circles." No real communication was taking place because the conversation lacked integrity.

If we want to have communication we must be honest and above board with one another. Again, we must create an atmosphere of trust. In this case, not trust in lieu of wrath, but trust in lieu of craftiness. None of us likes to be manipulated. It threatens our free will, and, in many cases our well-being.

Jesus told it the way it was. Not everyone liked

what he said; not everyone liked him. Others, however, never had occasion to fear that he was trying to manipulate them.

That's Far Enough

Fourthly, a nonthreatening conversation is one in which there is a respect for distance. While we have been saying a great deal about the need to be open in our relationships, we must acknowledge the fact that not everyone wants to be known to the degree that we wish to know him. We must not, therefore, attempt to coerce anyone into openness.

Perhaps you are irritated by the person who asks how old you are, or about your academic credentials, or your economic status. Maybe you inwardly object when a casual acquaintance calls you by your first name or teases you. You may dislike it when someone stands too close to you or touches you.

Why is this? Because the other person is not respecting distance. Uninvited intimacy threatens that little bit of privacy each of us tries to preserve for himself. Each of us has his own little inner sanctum into which he wishes no one to intrude. There are things we want no one else to know about us, even those nearest and dearest to us.

Eric Berne has educated us as to the games that people play. These are not the pleasant pastimes of children, but games with words that seek to help people get what they want. One such game involves styles of conversation that deal in the innocuous, ways of structuring and controlling communication in such a manner as to keep the spotlight off of us and on to others, or on the trivial. Why? With the aim in mind of keeping distance. That is the sole purpose.

Courtesy Is Called For

If we want communication we must let the other person set the limits of familiarity. A speaker is a guest on the doorstep of his listener. He will enter as bidden but will at all times conduct himself as company. He will view those rooms made open to him but will pry no door.

A high school junior remarked to his mother, "I am having three tests tomorrow." Immediately she said, "In what subjects?" It was intended to be an innocent inquiry but it was perceived as investigation. Immediately, he countered by saying, "school subjects," which was a way of saying nothing while saying something. If she had said, "That must mean a great deal of work for you," or "That must be of some concern to you," she might have learned more than by direct inquiry.

Communication is a very sophisticated matter. We practice it as amateurs and with failing results. We become frustrated, perhaps angry and isolated. May God give us the wisdom to talk to one another in such a way that we will want to keep on talking.

HELPS FOR STUDY

Goals

To grow in skill in talking with others in a non-threatening way and in a conscious spirit of Christ.

To foster a spirit of trust in our relationships.

Questions to Discuss

1. How can we express love and acceptance for a person

117

on one hand and needed judgment and guidance on the other hand?

2. How can we be sure we are free from manipulating people in our contacts with them and in efforts at winning persons to Christ?

3. What is meant by "proper distancing" between persons? How important is it to give attention to this?

4. What are the most important ingredients in building an atmosphere of trust?

Learning Activities

1. Discuss: What are signs that one person trusts another? (Openness, honesty, relaxed relationships, expressions of love and concern.)

2. Get in a conversation with two or three others on the subject of how we can build greater atmosphere of trust with each other?

3. Identify and work at some of the barriers to trust that come up between people. Talk these over with others: Denunciation, distance, lack of courtesy, manipulation, signals of unconcern and disinterest, unreliability, and others.

4. Find someone you have full trust in and express your confidence to that person. Consider what part Christian love plays in this relationship.

Love Makes The Word Go Round

IN *Company of the Committed* Elton Trueblood disturbs us with these words, "No person is really a Christian at all unless he is an evangelist or getting ready to be one."[1] If that statement is true, how many of us does it un-Christianize? Of course, we can argue about what is evangelism and, hence, who is an evangelist. Even so, it would require an awfully broad definition to take in some of us. The follower of Jesus Christ has signed up for a crusade, and he deludes himself if he expects to stay at home. Evangelism is implicit in discipleship and far more than we are willing to admit we know it is true. Consequently, we will breathe a lot easier when we get on with it.

Everyone an Evangelist

Paul was an evangelist. There was no evangelistic organization which bore his name, but day by day, nearly hour by hour, he did the work of an evangelist even as he admonished his pupil, Timothy, to do. Paul did not hide behind this argument that some are sowers

---

[1] Elton Trueblood, *Company of the Committed* (New York, N.Y.: Harper Publishers, 1961), p. 70.

and some are reapers then apologize for being a sower. He was a sower but he was also a reaper. And it is how Paul attempted to do the reaping that provides us a model for personal evangelism. Of particular interest to us here is his encounter with Festus.

Right at the start we should note that Paul apparently did not win Festus to Christ. In a way that should console us, for if we take seriously this matter of personal witnessing it is quite likely we too will not gain a commitment from everyone. This is no reason to think of ourselves as failures. Paul's experience with Festus did not discourage him.

This Is My Story

Now that we have said that, let us look at how Paul went about his work. One thing is immediately evident: Paul told his own story. He shared his personal witness. The Apostle talked a great deal about two people—Jesus Christ and the Apostle Paul—and usually he talked about them in relationship to each other.

There are thirty-two verses in the twenty-sixth chapter of Acts. The first twenty-three are given over to Paul's testimony. It is a forthright and detailed account of his conversion. The whole story is there. Paul the sinner is there. Paul the believer is there. Paul's text is his dialogue with Jesus on the Damascus Road. Not a bad text. His intentions were not in the least subtle. Agrippa picked this up in a minute and said, "You think to make me a Christian." To this charge Paul would have pleaded guilty instantly. This is one charge no Christian ever needs to be ashamed of. He needs only to be ashamed that it is not often enough brought against him.

Seeing and Saying

The most incredible question you can ask about witnessing is, "What in the world would I say?" What does a ten-year-old boy say when he comes home from the circus after having seen a lady in pink tights swept up into the air in the trunk of a giant elephant? He says what he saw! That is what witnessing is all about. The Bible calls it making known "the things you have seen and heard." No eloquent speech can ever be as effective as the simple testimony, "Once I was blind, but now I see." I think it might come as a great shock to some people to learn that conversions were taking place before the formulation of the Four Spiritual Laws. How did it happen? People witnessed to their own experiences in Christ.

After listening to a young man tell of a marvelous transformation that had taken place in his life as a result of receiving Christ as his personal Savior, I asked him how he had started on this new way. His previous life had been ruled by hate and lust. Now, here he was a radiant Christian, a preacher of the gospel of Jesus, and the pastor of a church. How in the world did it happen! Well, the explanation is simple enough. So simple, in fact, it was the least indelible portion of his story. As I recall he was working in a factory many miles from his place of birth. A fellow employee, his personal friend, had been converted through efforts of a Church of God congregation in the area. Consequently, the friend invited him to attend a revival

121

meeting. Since the friend was so lavish and enthusiastic in his praise of Christ this young fellow was constrained to go and find out for himself. He was likewise convinced to forsake his sin and follow Christ.

We Have Something to Share

He who disparages his testimony depreciates the grace that has been given him. It is unfortunate that so many of us do indeed minimize our own personal conversion experience to the degree that we are reluctant to share it. Beloved, that is as unforgivable as for a bride-to-be to hide the engagement ring on her finger in the presence of her friends because the diamond is small. The diamond is not important, be it large or small; the betrothal is important. It is the love of that man for that woman and that woman for that man that makes the ring significant, not the size of the diamond. Likewise, it is the fact that Christ loved you and gave himself for you, and that you responded to his gift, that makes your testimony significant. It is not the monumental transformation that took place in your life.

We have not taken ourselves off the hook by declining to witness because as we say, "My testimony is so ordinary." That does not explain why Barnabas was as much under orders as Paul. Has it ever occurred to you that God needs a lot of very ordinary testimonies, because there are more people like you to be converted than any other kind?

One of the most effective personal witnesses I have ever known I suspect of never having a mean bone in her body. She is one of those Nathanael-like persons in whom there seems never to have been any guile. She is the kind of woman who if she sees a stray cat in the neighborhood will put out a saucer of milk. Any little waif of a boy or girl could claim her fortune in a minute with a winsome look. If she ever got angry at you she would pray down so many blessings on you, you would want her to stay mad forever. And yet without an extraordinary deliverance from sin, she has a powerful witness for Jesus Christ. It is almost impossible to spend as much as five minutes with her, even if she has never seen you before in her life, without her sharing her faith with you.

Speak Up Anyway

Returning to Paul, we see further that he was willing to seem brash. One of the most powerful tools the enemy has for silencing our witness is the fear of being misunderstood. After listening to Paul's testimony, Festus displayed a deplorable lack of understanding or appreciation for the words that he had just heard. Paul had spoken from the depth of his heart, only to hear these cruel words, "Paul, you are mad. Your great learning is turning you mad." How would you feel after a put-down like that? But that is it, isn't it? We are afraid that if we witness to Christ we too will be thought to be crazy, religious fanatics.

A man who knows what he has is not shaken if somebody mislabels it. The Apostle Paul did not respond to Festus by saying, "Yes, you are right. I am making a silly fool of myself." But instead, he answered, "I am not mad, most excellent Festus, I am speaking the sober truth." That reminds me of Peter

123

on the day of Pentecost. Observers mocked, "These people are drunk." That didn't disturb Peter. In a loud, clear voice he explained that those spoken of were not drunk. They were filled with the Holy Spirit in keeping with the prophecy of Joel.

Private Language

Witness may communicate. Silence never can. Maybe the reason we are misunderstood is because we have not shared our faith often enough. We simply have not introduced people to the vocabulary of redemption. By our timidity we have developed a "mother tongue" which is spoken only in the church, as the language of immigrants may continue to be spoken in the home, whereas English is spoken elsewhere.

E. Stanley Jones called Rufus Mosely the most bubbly Christian he had ever met. Someone else said of Mosely, "The first time I heard him, I thought *he* was crazy. The second time I heard him, I knew *I* was crazy."

The obsession to be thought well of by all men is fatal to any effective Christian witness. The moment we allow ourselves to be preoccupied with what people will think of us if we speak of Christ we are destined to failure. If we are guilty of this, serious questions must be raised about whether indeed Christ is Lord of our lives. Where he is really preeminent there is no room for inordinate self-concern.

You Will Feel Good About It

Witnessing has to come under the category of "if

124

you know these things, happy are you if you do them."
Many people probably relish witnessing no more than
they do the exercise that prompted Jesus to give us
those words. But there is no way you can witness without feeling good about it. Even if you are made to feel
badly by the rebuttal of those to whom you witness,
you are made to feel good by the Master's comforting
words, "Well done, thou good and faithful servant."

A cab driver told some of us how he had shared the
claims of Christ with Art Linkletter on the streets of
downtown Dayton, Ohio. To his apparent surprise and
obvious joy, Mr. Linkletter was both receptive to and
responsive to his witness. Now you and I might question the sanity of speaking so openly of one's faith to
a celebrity. However, the cabbie felt constrained by
Christ and refused to be intimidated by an excess
concern for propriety.

From the Heart

Perhaps the most significant thing about this story
of Paul's defense is the depth of the apostle's feelings.
He displayed a true concern for others when lesser
men would have thought only of themselves. It is
utterly impossible for us to communicate the gospel
effectively if we do not do it at the feeling level. It
simply cannot be a sterile, academic presentation.
It certainly dare not be a holier-than-thou judgment
upon those to whom we witness.

Paul's fluent testimony is not to be confused with
the race-horse presentation of an auctioneer who cares
only to say, "Going, going, gone." As we listen to the
apostle speak to Agrippa, we hear some of the most

125

heartfelt words in all of the New Testament. He says, "I would to God that not only you but also all who hear me this day might become such as I—except for these chains." Paul made Christianity sound like a postcard from somebody in Miami Beach to somebody in Minneapolis, Minnesota, on the coldest day of winter, "Having a great time; wish you were here." And he meant every word of it!

We best share our faith when we feel very good about that which has happened to us and very badly that it has not happened to others. Joy without concern is a runaway engine; concern without joy is a disconnected caboose. We must get the two of them together. Not only could Paul say to Agrippa, "I wish everyone had what I have," he could also say to the Romans, "I could wish that I myself were . . . cut off from Christ for the sake of my brethren" (Rom. 9:3). The essence of effective witness is loving Christ and loving the lost. Love makes the word go 'round. The church cannot cease to love the world and hope to win the world.

We once invited a young man to speak at our church who had had great success in winning students to Christ, phenomenal success. His pastor said that it was not unusual for this young man to go with holes in his shoes in order to have money to spend entertaining the young people whom he sought to win to Christ. That's feeling!

A Word at the Right Time

We do not always know who is weighing the matter of commitment. Our witness can make the vital difference in such cases. The spokesmen for evil and doubt are never reticent to speak. How can we in the name of discretion abandon those who need our support and by default give them over to those who will aggressively misdirect them? Many of us are Christians today because someone tipped the scales for us when we were inwardly locked in debate. How priceless their gift: a word of encouragement, a deed of kindness, perhaps an invitation or maybe even gentle persuasion. Do we not owe the same to others?

Samuel Grafflin writes about a man who lived out his life in a small midwestern town. He was a nobody, a most inconspicuous man with little education. Yet, he was the most loved man in that small town. He was the one others came to when they needed someone to pray for them. They sought him out when they needed encouragement or moral direction. It is said that the day he died the shops did little business and there was a hush in all the streets. The rich man in town who had just taken delivery of a new carriage went personally to offer it for the use of the grieving widow. The county undertaker drove fifteen miles over the hills to offer his services free. As he said, "I was a drunkard on these roads until one day Joe got hold of me and told me of the saving grace of Christ."[2]

There is no greater ministry of love than to lead another person to Christ. Never let your love stop short of that.

[2]As retold by J. Wallace Hamilton in *Ride the Wild Horses*, p. 37.

HELPS FOR STUDY

Goals

1. To become involved in the work of evangelizing as an expression of Christ's love.

2. To take steps in developing a life-style that has sharing good news at its heart.

Questions to Discuss

1. Some people seem called to be soul-winners while others have different responsibilities in the kingdom of God. Is that a true distinction? Or, is there a sense that all are meant to evangelize?

2. What is the most appropriate style of sharing for you personally? In what sense does each person witness and evangelize according to his own style, skill, and opportunities rather than according to some general pattern? Of what value is a general pattern for personal witness?

3. What if a person just doesn't feel like sharing enthusiastically about Christ? Does that mean he is not where he should be in his Christian life? Does it speak of differences in personality?

Learning Activities

1. Stage some small event or tell some good news in as dramatic a way as possible in front of a group studying this course.

2. Ask the observers or hearers to share the story of what took place with someone else.

3. Analyze what happened in the process of sharing—varying personal viewpoints, differing skills and levels of enthusiasm in sharing.

4. Discuss how this all applies to sharing the good news of Jesus Christ.

5. Commit yourself afresh to the sharing style of Christian life.